LaZebnik, Laurice,
Strongheart : a dog who was a coward /

Eastern Branch
Jackson District Library   10/18/2018

STRONGHEART
A Dog Who Was A Coward

by
Laurice LaZebnik

© 2013 Laurice LaZebnik, Copyright Pending

LauriceLaZebnik.com |

All rights in this book are reserved.
No part of the book may be used or reproduced in any
manner whatsoever without written permission.
Send inquiries to laurl@sbcglobal.net

Fiction, Dogs, Native American, First Nation

ISBN 978-1482336368

Cover design and page layout by
Jennifer Hauschild | Hauschild-Design.com

Feather illustration by Samantha Hauschild

Cover photo by Jeff Steers

*This book is dedicated to
Ruben, Alena, Ruben Jr. and Israel Felhandler,
Cubans who dared to dream and found the
courage to create a better life.*

My friends, you have the strongest hearts of all.

Acknowledgments

*I am grateful for the friendship and support given
by the Columbia Women's Writers Group,
especially Jean Lantis and Ann Green
who read and re-read my manuscript over and over.*

I am amazed at the patience of my husband, Bob LaZebnik.

*I thank Cathy Drummands for her companionship,
for teaching me about the OES, and for blessing me
with three loving dogs who have lengthened my life
with their unconditional love.*

*I especially thank Herbie the Love Bug,
the reason for this novel.*

STRONGHEART, *A Dog Who Was A Coward*

FOREWORD

"Dogs are full of mysteries and secrets…(have) a way of thinking that only other dogs understand…a secret language…a different picture of the world hidden in their genes."[1] Compared to dogs, humans are hearing-deaf and scent-blind.

Dogs communicate with us…if we take the time to listen, and to watch. They can use sign language, vocalization, body postures and signals like facial expressions to send messages. I swear my dogs are telepathic.

Some hounds are more empathetic than some humans I know, and can match moods with mine. Studies show dogs use their intuition to detect illness, cancer, or epileptic seizures. They can smell ketones on a diabetic's breath when their sugar is low. Some know several hours before an ailing human will die, or the earth will shake. Dogs are used commercially to detect chemical markers for bed bugs, mold, peanuts, drugs, and explosives.

Some of the story of *Strongheart* comes from my observations during twenty years of caring for Old English sheepdogs, some from scientific research, and some is drawn from the depths of my imagination.

---

1 *Do Dogs Dream?* Stanley Coehn, W. W. Norton Publishing

STRONGHEART, *A Dog Who Was A Coward*

ONE

"Elizabeth, don't let that pain-in-the-neck scratch the pantry door!"

"Just watch him, Bob. See how clever your birthday present is? See how he's pawing it open? Did you see how he did that? He's opened the closet and found his leash. Watch how he gets the leash down."

"Come on, Elizabeth. That's impossible. The hand loop is hanging over the hook."

"Watch this. Did you see him jump? I knew he was smart when I saw him at the kennel. He's got it. Did you see that? He snapped his head to one side to dislodge the leash in mid-jump. Did you see that, Bob?"

"No, I can't watch that animal all day like you do...got a pile of papers to read. I've got work to do." Bob grumbles and rattles his newspaper. "Get real, Elizabeth. That dog isn't clever. He accidently bumped the leash before it fell."

"Oh yah? Then why is he bringing it to you?"

"Get that filthy rope off my lap," Bob wrinkles his face and flicks his hand at me like I'm a flea. "Get away from me, beast!"

"Bob!" Elizabeth frowns.

"I don't walk dogs." The man flings my leash to the floor and grabs his baseball cap from the table. "Honey, let's go outside. I want to show you something."

The round man leans down and whispers to me. "You are the bane of my existence. I said I don't walk dogs and I mean I don't walk dogs." He pauses mid-step, his hands on his hips. "Stop staring at me, Herbie. I'm warning you…one of these days I'm gonna grind you up and stuff you inside a sausage."

There he goes again. Earlier today this alpha told me he would turn me loose on a country road to see if I was clever enough to find my way home. I don't trust the guy towering above me. He gets angry fast and explodes without warning. The thing is, I lack the courage or muscle to stop him. One of these times he may come between me and Elizabeth.

Bob's wife makes life bearable for me in my new pack. If she turns against me I'm out of here. I'll run away…find the road back to my kennel. Bob will be sorry for the day he messed with one of Ken-Bear's sheepdogs.

Until I moved here I trusted the alpha of my family. My sire didn't dress up like a bird and strut around like he was a champion, which he was. My dam was soft like Elizabeth. She said a dog can usually read a person if he can see their eyes. She warned me to be wary of human males who shadow their faces with duck bills.

"Get over, dust mop," Bob says, chewing words as he walks down the dock. "You're going for a swim if you don't give me some room." His eyes flash annoyance. "Puppies drown in this lake every day." He stops near the end.

See what I mean? He calls me insulting names. His foot is edging me dangerously near the blunt end of this cedar plank pier. The guy is dominating the end of the dock. Where am I supposed to stand? If I twitch, I'll fall in.

"Take it easy on Herbie," Elizabeth says to Bob. "He's only a puppy, and there, see that? He's exposing his belly to you. I think that means he's submitting to you as the alpha. Thank goodness he can't understand what you say."

They don't get it. I'm not deaf and my nose works just fine. I can understand every word they both say, well, almost every word. I learn new ones each day because I watch a lot of television when they're gone. It's annoying when they talk about me like I'm not here.

If this unremarkable man would take the time to learn my language he may be able to explain why the dogs on television don't come down to play with me. The old grouch gets irritated when I bother him during a movie. He's a sourpuss… so sour he could make a mosquito's picker pucker. Yah, I know. He's the big boss in the house, my alpha.

"Be careful, honey. The puppy can't swim," Elizabeth says, bending down to scratch my scruff.

I think I'm going to love this female.

"He better keep his wet whiskers off my new loafers," Bob says as he admires his shoes and tweaks the bill of his cap against the late afternoon sun. "Elizabeth, there is no room to pet him here. I don't want to fall in the lake. And you're wrong about him. All dogs can swim." Bob clears his throat. "He's hardly a puppy. He's almost three months old." He blows his nose and jams his handkerchief deep into a pocket "That little beast has grown like a dandelion this past month, probably from chewing my socks, my slippers, and the leg on my green leather chair." He frowns. "Today I found his hair in the breakfast butter." I watch Bob curl his arm around her waist. "He's too much dog for you to be lifting. He must be 40 pounds…too heavy for a lap dog. How big will he get?"

"Fifty to a hundred pounds," Elizabeth says.

Bob's chin drops. He squints down at me but addresses Elizabeth. "Did you hear that? He's growling at me again."

I feel the wind picking up as he pushes his foot against mine. What did this old grumbler do…wake up this morning and say, "Today I'm gonna ruin a dog's life?" I'm worried that he will push me in the lake. I'm worried by the weather at Clark Lake, but I'm even more concerned by the way this man's mind works. I wouldn't be surprised if the winters are as dangerous here at this lake as he is. If I can take the brutal weather, I should be able to outsmart this alpha trying to dominate me, and any other tormentor lurking in my future.

"Fish feet!" He's nudging me with his shoe again. "I was here first," I growl, low enough to show respect yet serious enough for him to protect his backside. "I am not a beast. I am just an ordinary, well-bred animal. I'm not an ill-mannered wild dog." I push back.

"Herbie, get off my foot!" The thug twists his lips like he's sprouting aggression. "Elizabeth, get him to stop, or he's going in!"

"Look here old man, I found a chigger in my paw and I would rather not repeat the experience. I'm not going into this lake," I growl.

"Bob, Herbie's trying to tell you something."

"Yah! He wants to tear my leg off. Did you hear him snarl at me that time? We can't have a mean dog around here. Maybe you can get your money back. If he bites someone, we could get sued and lose everything. Elizabeth, he's leaning on my leg. Get him to move or I'm warning you, the dog is going for a swim."

Explaining to this signal-disabled man that I recognize him as the alpha in our pack, yet will defend myself against him if he backs me into a corner, is like pushing a river uphill. He's impossible. I don't know what Bob has against me…I didn't steal the meat from his bowl. Since I've come to live here he hasn't shown enthusiasm for much of anything, except for finding fault, nagging, and gloating. Know what I like about him? Nothing.

Elizabeth knows how to love a dog. She treats me naturally, like I'm a creek flowing downhill, the way water is supposed to flow. This woman gets it.

"Herbie, honey," she says. "Hold still."

The wind is picking up. I watch waves splash against the seawall. My mind drifts. I think of home. My sire told me that if I used my brains and showed respect to the alpha of my pack, love would come to me. I've tried using father's wisdom on Bob, but this guy is hopeless. I'm doomed for life, trapped with these people like a nut inside a shell.

When I look up I see a bully with the stomach contours of an ingested beach ball. Looking out I see a wave crest in the lake next to the dock. Looking down I see a long silver fish swish from under the dock, hover for a bit, and then dart into a swaying mass of seaweed. It looks like the fish I saw on the television Elizabeth plays for me when she leaves me alone.

"Look Bob," Elizabeth points to the water. "See that animal. I think it's a muskrat."

"Where? Oh, I see it now. Have you checked Herbie for mange?" He nudges me with the toe of his shoe. "Can humans get mange? Can I get it from this dog?"

"Don't be ridiculous. Ken-Bear's kennel has never had a case of mange. Bob, where is the puppy?" She scans the yard behind her. "Herbie honey, come!"

"So he's your honey now?" Bob points down at me. "The mutt's right here." He pulls his shoe from under my bottom as he changes position.

I snap a look to check his intention. All I see is stomach.

"I don't like the way this dog looks at me or the way he's moving his jaw." Bob shivers and pulls up his collar. "I think you'd better call and have the furnace checked for winter," he tells Elizabeth. "What does the beast want? Stop pawing me!"

I give up on moving his leg and turn my attention to this autumn day, the best afternoon for sidewalk sunning I've had all season. It's been warm and is cooling down nicely as the sun settles. The dog next door told me the weather can turn cold suddenly. Air, musty with decaying leaves, has become heavy with ash that steams a fog across the neighborhood.

I sense a change in the breeze over the choking smoke from the neighbor's smoldering brush fire. Fresh air grows crisper when the wind changes and comes from the north, a refreshing chill for a sheepdog with as much coat as I carry. I sense my world changing with the smoke that's being pushed out over the lake by these cool gusts and the seaweed being pulled by the current below.

"My beautiful hostas," Elizabeth says to Bob. "They're gone; the deer have browsed them to stubble. What do you want to eat? I'm getting cold. The Country Store is having a big sale on annuals. How about liver and onions for dinner tonight?"

I tip my head to look interested, but I'm not. The woman talks like a snake in tall grass. It's hard to track her slithering trail of thoughts. She's certainly smart enough to back up an idea with another of the same theme, yet she changes course and is on to a new topic before she reverses direction and makes a point with the first. One time she had a burr caught in her sock. She finished planting tulips, and then scratched her leg until it bled instead of removing the burr with her teeth when she found it.

"Elizabeth, this dog is driving me nuts. He's sitting on my foot again."

"Having Herbie near me makes me feel safe when you're away on business trips. We did finish obedience class..."

"Did your instructor teach you to wake me when you get out of bed each morning so you can walk the dog? Did you learn you must brush him for an hour each evening instead of curling up on the couch with me? Did he insist you pet him each time you pass him in the house or hurry outside each time he barks? Elizabeth, the dog trained you."

I can hear their gurgling laughter over the crash of the waves. I think obedience class was a waste, too. I wish Bob would like me as much as he seems to like Elizabeth.

"Sweetheart," Elizabeth says, "if you love this lake so much, why won't you swim with me?"

"The water's too cold. I'll swim when the lake gets above 90 degrees. Hey look!" He tightens one arm around Elizabeth's waist and points with the other. "A meteor!" Together they scan the blinking sky. "Make a wish," he tells her. "The next shooting star will seal your wish with luck." I see his shoulders heave. "Damn it, Herbie. Move off my foot!"

I peer out over the lake to watch yellow moonbeams flicker over wave swells. I'm teetering on the pier's edge as I admire my reflection in the water. I notice the animal Elizabeth calls a muskrat. It darts between swells of waving seaweed. My balance is precarious, yet I lean out to see where it has disappeared. That's when Bob pulls his other shoe from under my rump.

My next breath finds me toppling towards the water. My head hits first followed by a painful smack on my back. "Frog feathers!" I yelp in the underwater. "I can't swim!"

TWO

My paws float above me as I sink below the surface. Why isn't anyone saving me? I'm a puppy. Water is seeping between my teeth. I can't breathe down here.

My panic is replaced by curiosity. This underwater is cool, quiet and rather beautiful in the light from the moon. I'm feeling calmer, yet sense danger, and I'm not alone.

"Herbie? Herbie!" Elizabeth bellows. Her voice wavers, muffled by the water above. "Bob, where is our puppy?"

I can see their images wobbling over me through the waves. Bob is leaning forward, squinting and staring straight down at me. He's already off balance when Elizabeth reels around and bumps him with her hip. The old man falls forward, and I see him splash through the rippling surface.

"Bob," Elizabeth says, her voice barely audible, "You were supposed to be watching him." It sounds like I'm listening with a hair plug in my ear. "You said he was by your foot a minute ago." Her image is blurry. She's scanning the shoreline. "No, I'm not sure all dogs have the instinct to swim. Find him!" she screams.

I'm sinking fast. The moon beams a flickering funnel of light into the cloudy underwater where I find myself snarled in green slime. My heart is leaping like a frog after a fly. I try to remember which way is up when I see Bob thrashing about in sea reeds beside me. One glance and I know he can't help me. I struggle toward what I think is the surface when

I see what looks like a puppy hiding behind seaweed. Or is it a snake?

You! says the creature. *Come. I will show you something.*

The animal-snake-thing looks larger as it swims closer, like creatures do when I'm watching television. Could it be here to help me? "Let go of my foot!" It's dragging me deeper. My chest feels tight, like it will burst. Instinct tells me to wrench my paw from the predator's powerful claws and paddle hard with my legs. The ogre hovers behind the seaweed.

"Ouch!" It clamps my foot again. This is not the animal I saw from the dock. This is not the snake that hides behind the woodpile. Its muzzle moves next to mine. It has legs like mine, a body like mine and a head almost like mine. As quick as a rattlesnake's strike it snatches my other paw. I yank it back. "Stop it! Let go of me!" The animal rolls its eyes, shakes its head then drops the foot. "Thank you," I think to him. In the beat of a heart the muskrat-snake-coyote-dog thing swishes into the fluttering forest of lake weeds and disappears.

My chest is a vacuum willing to inhale seaweed, sand, anything if I can't have air. I feel dizzy, ready to explode. I paddle toward a place where I can breathe when I feel another tug on my scruff. No! I can't withstand another attack. I can't hold my breath any longer. Is this the end for me?

I swivel to free myself from the creature and find Bob. His arm and legs thrash with no sense of direction. I can see his frenzied face. His eyes are bulging, flickering from side to side like he's lost. His cheeks are ballooned with breath. His lips are squeezed to a pucker. It occurs to me that this man can't swim; this man doesn't know his way back to the surface; this man is in deeper trouble than I am. He clamps an arm around my belly and hugs me…and I didn't think he liked me.

My anus twitches like it's about to suck me inside out. I'm out of air. Instinct calls for one last try, one final thrust with my back legs. Instinct hints I should follow the path of bubbles escaping from my nose. I surge upward with every bit of strength I have to make a path to the surface. I pass the bubbles.

The man clenching me is a drag. His struggle pulls me backwards. His free hand is reaching to grip something, to grab anything to save himself. My chest explodes as I break the surface. I fill my lungs, gasp, gag and cough. I'm still coughing when Bob's head emerges near mine. His free hand wraps around a dock post. I hear him struggle for breath. I feel him release his grip on me. I sense relief that I'm not dead. Instead of a sky above me pock-marked with stars, I see wood planks.

Elizabeth screams "Bob! Herbie's gone!"

Without losing grip on the metal pole, he reaches to where I am bobbing under the dock and jerks me to his side. Breathing hard, he says, "Here's your dog, Elizabeth," and shoves me to where she can see me. "You were right. The dog can't swim."

I'm about to bite the hand that holds me when I see one of Elizabeth's willowy arms reach down. She grabs me by my scruff like my dam did when I was a pup, and lifts me until my front feet grip the dock's edge. "One, two, three," she says and pulls the hair at my neck until I am on the planks.

"How did Herbie get into the water?" she says to Bob and hugs my dripping torso to her chest.

"It was an accident Elizabeth, honest," I hear him say from the lake below.

"No it wasn't. You knocked him in!"

"He jumped before he was pushed." Bob raises an arm for her help. "You should have tied that mutt to a tree when I told you."

Elizabeth stands with one hand on her hip, ignoring her husband. The other is cradling me. "If you knew how much I paid for this puppy…" Her screeching range is so high even birds become confused and crash into one another.

I'm thinking…why are they having a domestic drama now? We're all alive. These people must have horse feathers inside their heads.

"I saved him, didn't I?" Bob says with a snarl.

Now that's a fat load of nonsense. The man clearly choked. He wouldn't have the chops to save his own sire…if he had one.

"What's he growling about? I never wanted this dog or any dog," he says and raises his arm for Elizabeth's help again.

This is the man I'm bound to for life? This is the guy who lied about saving a dog he never wanted? Something is wrong inside this fellow's head. Maybe he ate some bad garbage.

Ignoring her husband's request for help, Elizabeth rubs my coat. I cough, snort, and sputter. I am as wet as a fish. She clutches me to her soft chest where I hear the same pounding coming from her heart that I heard from my birth mother's belly. Elizabeth doesn't smell as sweet as my dam, but she's warm and I feel safe with her. Life at Clark Lake would be okay if only that sick slug would get lost and live his life out in the underwater like that coyote-snake creature.

Almost drowned, I make an important decision. Before the water swallows me again, I will run away. I will return to my canine family where I am appreciated. I will live in a place where I will be safe from the creature in the underwater and safe from this insufferable man still floating in the lake.

"What about me?" Bob calls. An oily film from his hair dressing shimmers in the water around him. "Don't I count around here?"

"Of course you do, but you can swim. You're just wet. Come ashore and dry yourself." Elizabeth grasps the long white hair covering my eyes and twists it with an elastic band from her wrist. "There. Now you can see," she says to me. "You won't fall in the lake again. Come inside, honey."

"Shave the damn dog's head," Bob grumbles as hand over hand he makes his way along the dock and over the deep water until he can touch bottom near shore. Liquid squishes from his loafers as he climbs over the seawall and walks toward the cottage. Each step seems to stir his anger and stretch his once perfectly shined shoes. "I tell you, that dog is trouble on four feet." He strips before entering the cottage. His rumpled trousers form two perfect funnels for draining into his shoes. The echo of the kitchen door slamming and his sad laundry are all he leaves outside.

I'm standing by the counter next to his wife when he stabs his finger at me. "You! Wipe those muddy feet before you come into this house, and I better not catch you in my chair!"

I observe him waddle into the bedroom. The man has a lump of rolled fat around his middle and an ugly set of buttocks. He emerges a short time later wearing a robe and his new leather night shoes. I slide from his chair and scoot under the table where he can't reach me.

"You give that dog run-of-the-house and he picks my man-chair. Look! Is that blood on the leather?"

"It must be from Herbie's foot." Elizabeth kneels, pulls me from beneath the table and checks my paw. "You have a cut, and you've lost some skin, my poor puppy."

I lick the pain growing in my foot and taste salty blood. My paw pad has been barked like the tree at the end of the driveway, the same tree Bob rubs with the fender of his car when he shoots out each morning.

My alpha shuffles across the room in his polished leather slippers. "Elizabeth, there's a puddle next to my chair. It better be water." He bends down to look under the table. "How much did you pay for this mutt?"

"I meant to tell you," she says, and towels the pine planks dry. "He was sort of on sale because his coat is a little off-color and curly, but he has a formidable pedigree. He was the only pup left from a litter of six. His parents and grandparents are all champions."

"You mean those dim-witted breeders consider this pup worth less because of the color and curl of his coat? His hair looks fine to me." Bob's scowl recedes as he drops into his chair. He picks up the newspaper and opens it wide. I move beside Elizabeth.

"His breeder told me the Old English sheepdog line is supposed to have white and black straight-haired coats," Elizabeth says to the newspaper. "Adult hair turns gray and white. Herbie has some curly brown hair on his rump. Did you notice?"

The paper drops to his lap. He snaps me a look. "No." Up goes the newspaper.

"Show judges would disqualify this puppy because of his brown color. She told me we couldn't breed him unless his coat grows in gray."

"Why would anyone want to breed him?" He rattles the paper as he turns a page.

"She says a defect like that can be passed on to the next generation."

Down goes the newspaper. "Look Elizabeth, color makes no difference to me. He's the same amount of trouble brown and white as he would be gray and white." Up goes the paper.

Understanding that my alpha wants to kill me on the same day I discover I have a major breed defect puts my self-image into a spin. Add that an underwater animal has tried to drown me, and what little puppy confidence I have plummets. Each time I see Elizabeth's glance drift my way I can feel her eyes singe the brown hair on my backside. I hate being imperfect.

When I venture outside for my last relief for the day I drag my bottom on the lawn to make the curls go straight, and then squat under a low bush so the owls can't see my imperfections. I try to sleep, but my mind races over endless plots to blot my birthmarks. I'm pulling out the unnatural tie Elizabeth has stretched around my top knot when I hear Bob call from inside.

"Look. See him drag his butt? He's got worms."

"Stop it, Bob. You've insulted Herbie." She holds the door open. "I think he's pouting."

I am not pouting. I'm planning. A prophecy from my sire slips into my mind. It was the day I left Ken-Bear's kennel. "Number four," he said. "I expect greatness from you." Father should have known I could never be a champion; after all, he is in the breeding business. What could he have meant by greatness? Unlike those in my pedigree, it appears I must excel outside the show ring.

As I watch my new family ready themselves for sleep it occurs to me that I may have made a mistake in the underwater. If I had acted on my anger when I panicked and went a trifle mad, if I had ripped Bob's arm off at the elbow, he would have had the opportunity to survive or not on his own. Bob's ability to swing at me with only a stump would be an advantage for me, and then I might have had half a chance to survive.

But my animal instinct had warned me not to disfigure him. Horseflies will not bite Bob's sour hide. Flies never land, just hover in his presence. Instinct always knows.

THREE

Calle O'Riley possesses more authority and more power in the animal kingdom than any dog I have met or ever will meet. The leader of our regional pack no longer needs to charge to the high ground to take her rightful place, no longer needs any animal's approval on hard decisions for our neighborhood, and no longer needs to deny she's done some heinous act if she were to be accused. Lake dogs know not to cross this Irish setter. They respect Calle for her knowledge and for her position in the pack. She remembers everything. They have given her loyalty and a place on the history trees. I didn't know this when I first arrived at Clark Lake, when I was afraid of that creature in the underwater and of my alpha, when I was alone and needed a friend the most.

My education begins during the month for shooting stars, the season when the moon sleeps the shortest time before the round August sun awakes to roast the day. I stand by the fence separating our yards and wait, stomping my feet to stay awake, killing time before dawn by watching fireflies light up the lawn. The sunrise slips up behind Calle's sleeping mound of red fur.

I pace, paw the grass, lower my chest, and scoot my front legs straight out along the turf…a move any dog knows is an invitation to play. No reaction. Not even a blink. I jump in place to spark her interest, bark, strut, and make a mid-air twist. Nothing comes from the hound huddled on the other side of the braided wire fence. I repeat my invitation with play-bows. The red dog remains as still as a stone, except for her twitching tail.

Her apathy fuels my frustration, progresses into my pestering, and explodes into boisterous barking. "Is anybody there?" And louder still, "Is anybody at home inside that red head?" I want to squeeze the attention bone behind her eyes. I escalate my rhythm and amplify my volume until my own ears hurt, and then wait in the sultry, fly-buzzing silence.

Throughout my antics the red dog stares ahead. From time to time she flicks her mouth to catch an insect that has landed on her snout, then goes back to what seems to me like stargazing. But all the stars are gone and the sky is red.

I am feeling outrageously ineffective, like a flea on a poison collar, when I remember my sire telling me I was born with a tool that could help me all my life…persuasiveness. He told me at times our breed must convince a nervous herd of sheep to take an unfamiliar path to safety. I've never herded sheep, but I think that convincing another dog to do my bidding couldn't be all that difficult. I take a deep breath and try again. I paw the grass and pitch divots of sod skyward. My howl shakes leaves from trees. Fish float belly up. Flies drop dead in mid-air.

The response from the red setter is a slow turning of her head, then a quick look away when I catch her eye. I feel slighted. I'm beginning to doubt my powers as a herding dog, but blame the insensitive setter so I'll feel better about myself. This red dog is snooty. This old bitch is mean.

Without warning the lounging setter heaves forward, stretches back, arches her spine and pushes her front feet straight out. She propels what looks like tired bones into a sitting position and stands.

"Hello," I bark.

Without a glance she turns her back to me and pads away from the fence. Near her doghouse Calle curls around like a cut-worm and turns her head to glance my way. Our eyes meet. I hold my breath. At least she has reacted. I try an insult. "Hey red dog, you act like a stuffy, purebred from champion stock."

Her tail wags broadly as she says, "The wisdom of old age will always outdo youth and skill."

So, she is laughing at my inexperience. I'm lonely and have too much to ask of her to be angry. Questions explode over the fence and across her yard. "What kind of animal did I see in the water?" I step closer to the fence. "Did it bite your foot too? Why did it attack me? I need to know. What is your name?"

"So many questions from such a young dog, are you sure you don't have one more?"

"Yes, I need to know how a firefly glows without burning its tail."

Before the red dog can toss the answers back across the fence she slides her head to one side and stares at something behind me. "Is your alpha at home today?" she whispers.

"Yes, but he's still sleeping inside the cottage. I feel so miserable out here without him this morning, it's almost like having him here." All of a sudden I catch the scent of the alpha of the Hartman household. I snap my head around. He is wearing blue pajamas and his new leather slippers.

"At seven o'clock in the morning dogs may not bark," Bob says as he hauls me home by my choke collar. "That's the way it's always been in this neighborhood and that's the way it will be with you. And Herbie, next time you make a snowstorm by chewing an entire box of tissues in front of the electric fan, I'll cut off your ears."

I drag all four claws in the turf out of protest. I can see the red dog watching. I squeeze my eyes shut and try to disappear from her view.

"To bark is trouble for you until after eight-thirty!" Bob yells loud enough to wake animals sleeping in the forest. "I know it was you who chewed the back seat in the station wagon. I'm going to pull out all of your teeth if you try that again."

FOUR

"Bob, stop!" Elizabeth warns.

I glance up. An automobile tire is rolling towards me.

"What?" Bob calls from the open window as the car comes to a stop.

"The dog! You're driving over Herbie!"

I'm frightened, too scared to move.

"What did you say?" He stops when Elizabeth screams again, cups his ear to hear and is attempting to back up when I muster enough courage to roll free. That man would have driven over me again.

"Are you wearing your hearing aids?"

"That's what I forgot. I'll come back and…"

"No. For the dog's sake, stop! He's still in the driveway. You'll back over him."

I told you he was trying to kill me. As I crawl off the driveway I growl at him, "That unclaimed dog turd in the upstairs hallway wasn't mine."

Bob roars the motor. The sound is so threatening I pee all the way down the driveway to the patio where Elizabeth stands. I slip behind her and peer out between her legs. She bends down and checks my ear.

"Lucky you," she says to me. "He only ran over your hair at the tip of your ear with his tire. Stay away from his car when he's driving and you'll be fine." She rubs the hair behind both ears and kisses my nose.

"Bob!" she shouts. "Don't leave for work without your breakfast. Come in right now. It's on the table." He stops the car and walks to the front door where I am still checking for wounds.

"I know it was you." he says as I pause over my empty water dish. "It was fresh, still soft. I stepped in it after my shower. It had to be yours."

"Okay, sir," I whine. "You are registering your disapproval and that's perfectly natural." My whine morphs into a growl. "What is unnatural is not lugging your fat carcass out of bed to let a dog outside when he scratches on your bedroom door in the dark. You are a selfish, insufferable alpha, and you lack an understanding of a dog's poop chute problems." I paw his leg. "Hey! Can't you see I'm thirsty?"

Later that same day I plod along the well-worn path beneath the forsythia bush. This hidden road skirts the end of the O'Rileys' woven wire fence, a barrier between or yards. It tracks under the honeysuckle bushes that were planted as a barricade against intruders...and stray dogs. I stumble up the steep hill, take my place on Calle's doghouse matt and keep my muzzle shut. For the first time in many suns a smirk forms on the red dog's face. It's almost a smile. She flips her chin and throws me a soft bark. "*Bojo.*"

I respond with a tip of my head…I don't understand. Her first word to me doesn't sound like language used by Old English sheepdogs. I tip my head to study her smile. It's not Irish setter, either. I'm confused.

"*Bojo* is a greeting in Potawatomi," she says, reading my thoughts as all dogs do with each other. I am wondering if Potawatomi is a new breed of canine when she answers before I can ask. "It is the name of a great tribe of humans who lived on this land many moons ago. Bojo can mean hello or goodbye." This red dog pronounces her words slowly, ignoring my next question about why she must think messages to me in strange tongues. "I name you Walks Like a Bear because you have earned the right to wear the name of bear. You were selected by the wolf in the lake and you escaped his grasp."

I'm dizzy with information. So the muskrat Elizabeth thought she saw was a wolf in the underwater and not a coyote or snake like I thought. I didn't know wolves could live underwater like the fish. My sire told me the wolf was the grandfather of all dog breeds. This doesn't make sense at all. I almost drowned in that underwater.

And now the Irish setter wants me to answer to another name. I have enough trouble with names and this is too much information. Ken-Bears is my first name and the name of the kennel where my family's trophies line the walls. Herbie is a name given me by Elizabeth. Hartman is the name of the alpha of my pack at Clark Lake. "Can't you just call me Herbie?" I give Calle a toothy grin. "My life is confusing enough."

She shakes her head. "Among the People of the First Nation, every newborn is given a name, the earliest of three he will wear over a lifetime. The first is a private name, from his Potawatomi family or clan. The second is taken after a dream in his youth or of some particular habit. The third name is earned after some accomplishment."

"I think Swims Like a Stone is a more appropriate name than Walks Like a Bear. And why are you, a dog, giving me a First Nation name? I was born in Monroe, Michigan earlier this season, before you met me. I was called number four. I'm not part of this Pottahoochimee pack."

"The tribes name is Potawatomi. Pot-ta-wa-to-mee. Next, you were chosen to be part of this Native American family because you drive us all crazy with your questions. You seem to be able to think and hopefully, someday, if we're right, you will be able to solve problems. I chose that name because you shuffle like a black bear," when she grins I can see she is missing teeth, "and because you have no tail. Neither does the bear. Your front shoulders are lower than your hind quarters, like a bear. I have the authority to name you because your future is before you. Mine is coming to an end."

"Why did you give me a Pot-ta-wa-to-mee name? Why you?"

The old dog's eyes smile shut. Her tone turns serious. "I am a dog who lives close to the earth, listens to the land, and tastes the lake. I have studied the smells of the wind, watched the movements of the birds and have been chosen for a special task by those before me. My job is to remember every legend and pass each one on at the right time. Most animals in our lake kingdom have heard the legends, but few remember. The crow is too flighty and remembers only her own history. The deer say they are too busy trying to find food and a safe place to sleep to remember deer tales. No animals think they need history until they get in trouble and need some wisdom. That's when they come to me to learn.

"Walks Like a Bear, as your body grows to fit your big feet, so will your spirit expand to fit your name. I expect that of you. I expect you to remember all that I tell you." The old setter guides my gaze with her glance. "I will explain in the language of signing that all understand because…" Thrusting one paw in a straight line from her mouth, she tells me that her speech is straight and truthful.

"What are you called?"

"I have three names. Calle is the name given me by my family pack. O'Riley is the name of my Clark Lake alpha. And, my Potawatomi name is Red Dog."

Suddenly shy, I fiddle with my paw pads. "I guessed your name would be Red Dog," I shake my chin and snot slides from my nostrils, "…because your coat is the color of the sunset."

"Now that is a staggeringly astute observation for a dog with such a disgusting nose drip. Wipe it with your paw, please." The Irish setter adjusts her frame, now bony with age, and yawns. "My name comes from the flames of the Three Fires Nation, the land around this lake where we live."

"Calle, do you know why the wolf tried to pull me into the underwater?"

Ask me, Walks Like a Bear.

I jump to my feet. "Who's that?" A voice I've heard before comes from behind. I see no one. "Calle, did you hear him?" I can feel my ears perk and the hair along my spine stand at attention.

"We are the only two in my yard," she says. Even Red Dog looks puzzled.

"Someone spoke to me. I've heard that voice before in the underlake. Calle, I'm afraid that wolf has come to pull me beneath the water again."

"Oh, of course. It's Wolf," she says.

"Do you mean the voice is the wolf in the underwater that hurt my foot?" I shift my head and sniff the air to locate the enemy but smell nothing unusual. "Where is his scent? How can he live under the water? Do you know him, Calle?"

"Stop trembling, he's here to help you. I've known him all my life," she says.

Walks Like a Bear, Wolf says.

"Pussy feathers!" I jump as his words tear into my mind. "Calle, there he is again. He speaks my name but I can't see him. If you've known him all your life, why can't you hear him?"

"Talk to him," Calle says. "Just think the words, but drop that disgusting language."

"I'm supposed to think words to an underwater wolf… polite words?"

"That's right."

It's going to be a short evening. "Calle, is he a real wolf, or is this a trick?"

Walks Like a Bear?

Okay. Okay, I'm trying. I'm trying to think the pictures. This way of thinking is a new experience for me and I'm still a puppy, so don't expect too much. I'm trying now. You have my full attention. *Hello. Hello Wolf. Are you still there?*

Learn the legends and remember them forever. I will teach you. Look at the Sycamore tree, Wolf says.

"Calle, he wants me to look at a Sycamore. Did you hear him? Which tree is that?"

The Irish setter nods toward a towering trunk with pealing gray bark. The leaves above are large enough to cover my ears.

When you see an owl in that tree, you must tell Red Dog, Wolf says.

"Did you hear that, Calle?"

"I haven't been able to hear him for some time," she says. "It's hard for me to hear anyone."

Besides being near deaf she forgets. She's old. Walks Like a Bear, focus on the sky. When a canoe comes from the clouds with twelve natives paddling and a barking dog at the bow, tell her.

"Okay Wolf, but I have thoughts about that. I'll remember this for my friend since she's almost deaf, but why me? Why are you talking to Calle by way of me?"

Focus on the forest. When you see a solitary hunter, bow in hand, followed by a pack of hounds, tell Red Dog.

"Why?" I think the question.

Wolf doesn't answer, but I can hear a sigh.

"Hello Wolf. Hello." I wait, but there is no answer. "Calle, has he gone?"

"Yes, if he doesn't answer."

"This wolf thinking inside my head scares me. I'm too much of a coward to let someone into my thoughts. I could get in a lot of trouble."

Calle hesitates. "Herbie, you are still a puppy. Courage can't develop if a pup has too much fear or is afraid to face change. You must learn from Wolf and from me. You will make mistakes. You can learn from your mistakes. Experience will help to ripen your courage. Listen, learn and remember. What the wolf says will change your life."

"I'm supposed to tell you when I see a canoe coming from the clouds with twelve native people paddling and a barking dog at the bow. That sounds silly to me."

"Wolf told you that?" Calle is silent for a long time. "So, the end of living is close. That cloud formation is a sign for me that time is short for the one who sees the vision or someone close to her. Walks Like a Bear, the sign in the clouds could be for you or it could be for me. It could be anyone, even Elizabeth." The temperature is dropping. The sky disappears in the dark. Calle continues in the same low voice she used when she named me."

"Bear is the most respected animal of the Potawatomi. Bear is clever. By day he conceals himself in hollow trees. Bear is crafty. He chooses beech nut trees near swamps so he can eat their nuts and travel the thick scrub by night to hunt for food. Bear is powerful. One power he owns that sets him apart from others in our kingdom is his ability to come close to death, to hibernate. When it gets cold like this," Calle shivers and feathers her long tail over her back, "Bear finds a cave on a hill or a hole in a tree stump, curls into a ball like we do, and sleeps until spring. When Bear enters the darkness, Bear speaks to the Great Spirit, then returns home to us to give directions. This is what our ancestors believed.

"Walks Like a Bear," Calle continues. "This is my place to stand, my yard. When you come into my wigwam, you must honor the spirit of Bear and show respect for me. When you are invited in, you must immediately lie down where I direct and take the same place whenever you visit. Once down look away and do not disturb my privacy. That is the custom of a guest when entering the home of a member of the First Nation."

"I'm not sure I can remember all this," I say and walk in circles next to the door of her doghouse. "May I go inside now?"

"Concentrate. You can remember. Wait for my invitation to enter. I call my home a wigwam to honor the homes of our ancestors. Respect is the key to living with others. This tradition became necessary among the Potawatomi because many animals and people lived in one room." She walks into her doghouse and continues. "You must not bark or howl unnecessarily." Red Dog arranges herself on the floor of her lodge, closes her eyes and nods her invitation for me to enter. "Walks Like a Bear, your world is only beginning. Much change is ahead of you. Every single being moves. Nothing stays the same."

I drop to her floor, following her lead, and squirm around with my mouth clamped shut. We lay there for what seems like forever before I blurt, "Calle, a bark is so hard to hold back. You must know that. Don't you ever bark at the moon?"

"Only when I'm happy," a grateful smirk slides down her muzzle, "or when I race the fields at night." Calle sticks her head out of her wigwam to check the weather. "Look. The sky is speaking. Do you see?" She motions with her muzzle and points to the red mass slitting the deep blue overhead. "We will have a great rain early tomorrow. The storm will be long and block the sun from warming our backs." She pushes straw into a mound near her entry. "This will keep the cold from biting my bones." She pauses to look my way. "You can learn to speak without words, my friend. We can look into each other's hearts. If you want to learn what I can remember of the ways of the Potawatomi, you may come after the next sun rises. There is so much I have forgotten. If another animal tells you a legend, remember it forever. You must remember. I'm counting on you. Bojo."

Just like that I am dismissed. Before standing I absentmindedly reach with my back paw to scratch my ear.

Calle sees the movement and a grin draws her jowls high. She stands and dips her head in appreciation. "Don't look so puzzled, Herbie. You have just made the sign in Potawatomi that means you have heard and understood." She lumbers around in a circle in the tradition of our species, one, two, three times. The old dog lies down in her nest, closes her eyes and is asleep before I can exit.

"Bojo, Calle," I whisper and back from her wigwam, being careful not to disturb her straw wall and let the rain in to bite her. As I trample the muddy trail home I wonder what the special task was that she had been given by those before her. I wonder where she acquired all her knowledge. Could it be she learned from the same wolf that is riding around inside my head? I wonder why people's minds are so dull. I remember everyone I have ever met and all their stories. I wonder if my wolf sometimes crawls into my alpha's thoughts.

Before I bark to be let inside my cottage, I walk like a bear to where Bob has parked his car and pee on the tire.

FIVE

Before the dark eats the blue sky away, Calle comes around the fence and stands beside me. Passing her paw along the entire vault of the sky, she begins where the daystar rises and ends where the daystar sets. She signs that for almost a full moon she had been listening to me crying the blues. "Being a moonstruck dog is not good for your reputation in our pack," she growls. "All animals know bear naturally have a *soongetcha*, a strong heart. Herbie, if you are heard sobbing during your day terrors, some may consider you a coward. You are insulting the spirit of Bear when you wail and are undeserving of your name.

"Even if a Potawatomi is fighting for his life," Calle continues, "he does not cry out. That would dishonor his life. It is all right to feel bad and howl but you must walk bravely and weep inside your cheek."

I rub my ears, embarrassed to look in Calle's direction, and I'm hungry. I feel my jaw slump until my black nose touches the ground. "I can't help it that I don't walk like I'm brave," I whimper. "It's an accident of birth that I walk like a bear," I whine. I'm finding it difficult to control the wail that is hiding inside my cheek. I look up and see ducks flying towards the marsh. My stomach hurts. Howls heave and twist deep inside my chest. "Calle, it's too hard to find courage. I don't think I'm old enough to be brave. I'm only a little dog, and I'm hungry. I miss my parents. I need someone to take care of me... feed me. I don't want to work this hard. I want to run away. I want to go back to Ken-Bear's kennel. I want my sire and my dam to do my thinking for me and keep me safe and warm."

Calle lies quietly beside me and listens to me blabber on and on. I tell her about losing some bones I stole and buried. At first sympathetic her eyes change to slits and a scowl forms on her forehead. It's a long while before she speaks.

"Saving food in a *cache* is natural and smart. Hoarding food or stealing food from another's winter store is not the way of the Potawatomi. A brave from the First Nation takes from nature only what he needs. Another creature's life may depend on eating one of the bones you took.

"Walks Like a Bear, in our clan of Potawatomi," Calle continues, "we believe both the good Bear and the evil one exist. Bear is so powerful and feared he is given the job of breaking barriers...fixing what has been broken. The legend tells of Bear pounding across the lower earth by rushing at a solid rock to create a channel. You might think of your destiny as changing what does not work or is harmful, always with honor and compassion for others. This great strength drawn from Bear's spirit can also be used for evil. You must choose your path." Using her low, steady voice to emphasize the importance of her words, Calle tells me to think about it. She stands and strolls home.

I don't know how to find the right channel. I don't even know how to find the wrong channel. I'm not sure I remember how to walk like a bear. I shake the hair from my eyes and wonder how Calle collected all this wisdom. I stand, stretch and wonder why my foot hurts. At home I find Bob's baseball cap behind the sofa. I wonder how long it will float.

SIX

"Where's that thieving hound?" a neighbor shouts as she bursts into our yard. "I know it's you," she points, looking directly at me. "I've already seen the Schmidts' police dog and that old dog the O'Rileys have. You are the only dog left in the neighborhood with big enough feet to fit the prints left behind in the snow. I'm reporting you to the dog catcher. What's your name?"

"Rover," I bark, and retreat under the forsythia bush. A blinding beam from the sun bounces off the empty pot she carries, a roasting pan with deep sides like Elizabeth uses to braise beef brisket.

The woman pauses to get her bearings, wipes her brow, and plows straight towards the front door. She's wearing a scarf wrapped around her head and a scowl on her face. "You!" She shakes her finger in my direction. "I see you under there, and I demand you stop relieving yourself on my lawn!" The short, rotund woman fumes as she fist pounds our front door.

* * *

This day had begun peacefully enough. Earlier, while I was walking, I caught the scent of fish entrails. My nose followed the odor to a compost pile where I discovered what was left of an entire school of decaying bluegills. I considered disguising my scent but remembered how embarrassed I had become the last time I rolled in dead fish. Elizabeth bathed me with lavender-scented soap, and then to mask the scent the neighborhood dogs urinated on me.

A little later, while I was at my front door and back to the routine of sunrise stirrings that set my days in motion, I barked the entry code and slumped to listen with my ear to the mail slot. The listen can be long at the narrow crack in the door. I waited.

Daily rituals occurred inside our cottage. The rush of flushing water was the first sound to float from the slot. Blasting water was followed by steam-hissing water. The aromatic stink of Elizabeth's bitter morning coffee seeped along the crack, followed by a grunting and the scraping sound. I saw her once squeezing her legs into stiff blue jeans. My neck cramped. Frog fur! My muscles flapped. Fish feet! They jerked…all from the angle of my slump. Spider spines! The door opened.

"Get out of the way, mutt," Bob said.

Happy to move and save my ribs from being crushed, I stepped aside and held my breath as the man with morbid bad manners opened his car door.

"I hate to see you go," Elizabeth called after him.

"I love to watch him leave," I whispered from the front door. The bloated wind bag's roaring engine droned out of range on the far curve of Clark Lake. The floating stench of warm rubber, motor oil, and boot wax cleared with the help of a strong lake breeze. As good as I felt from his absence, I was still skittish and far beyond my morning calm…long past my limit of patience with Elizabeth for our sunrise walk. I wanted to bite at her heels to make her move. I could easily have charged straight up those cottage logs like a bear to scare that sluggish worm of a woman out of the bathroom and chase her out this door.

Instead, I worked on developing patience and breathed deeply. Calle told me I have a foul mouth and must stop talking trash. She said a dog of my position in a household like this one should be respectful. I have no idea what that four-legged flea circus meant. What I need is diversion.

I clocked the speed of squirrels who shared my yard. Zip, my fastest friend, made it to the oak tree by the time I got to walnuts on my daily list of nuts. Lazy, a black squirrel, took her time. I got all the way to pecans in my chain of nuts before she reached the oak. She wouldn't live long if she took the same amount of time crossing the road as it took her to get to pecans. Some mornings Elizabeth appeared before macadamia nuts. Other mornings, she emerged after pistachios.

Today she appeared bundled against the weather so completely that all I could see were her blue eyes smiling in their sockets. While she strapped me into an old canvas backpack held on with Bob's red suspenders, she explained she had registered us for dog agility training. She slid a heavy weight into each side of the pouch mounted on my back.

"This heavy book is about training a dog for the show ring. And this volume is about child psychology."

My knees slumped from the weight.

"Ready? Set? Let's go!" she said before I could start the nut chain again.

My frustrations vanished as our march down the sunrise road began. This morning the air smelled odd. Besides feeling the weight on my back I sensed something different… something was so right and something else was wrong, or would be wrong and dangerous. I sniffed the air but couldn't determine where the trouble lurked. I noticed the red sky as

Elizabeth and I jogged. Calle would say the red sky signaled a great storm could come.

I sidestepped away from a burly dog cruising down the sunset road. His head was large and his teeth looked like the tines of a garden fork. He growled that he would rather disembowel me than sniff my butt. I increased my speed.

"The weather is mighty peculiar this year," Elizabeth told me. "We had an early fall, early ice, and early snow." She jogged ahead while I stopped, sniffed the air, and caught the smell of roasted red meat.

The succulent scents stirred my soul and fed my wildest dreams. Juicy meat on crispy bones are as rare as graveyards to canines like me who have highly regulated diets. My nose led me to a shining roasting pan of browned backbones and rounded shinbones with holes the size of moonstones… chunks of crunchy tenderness. I scanned the landscape and found I was all alone with rib-bones baked golden, their hollows filled with umber marrow. I found knucklebones with bits of browned flesh still meshed in crisped cartilage webs.

I placed my paw on the meatiest wished-for-bone and considered that few dogs could walk past a jawbone without mouthing it. Fewer still could drag home a collarbone, or one of the thighbones. Making a decision to take them all was the easy part. Savoring bones took chewing. Chewing took time. Elizabeth would be calling for me soon. The most exquisite bone, a marrow-filled shinbone, was my first choice. I lifted it from the pan, but discovered I craved the roasted rib bone, a bone too large for my mouth. The shinbone dropped.

Elizabeth whistled. I kicked the shinbone along the pavement, grasping the rib bone between my teeth, all the while trying to decide which bone to grab next. I pulled Bob's red suspenders free. The backpack swung low enough to slip in a rib bone. A hickory nut tree in a snow bank caught my eye.

I dug a depression in the snow near the trunk, packed in the shinbone, and ran back for more.

Elizabeth's second whistle ripped a hole in the air. I stuffed the backpack with small bones, scraped some loose snow over my *cache*, and sprinted to catch her… the backpack straggling behind.

I passed a house where an elderly Labrador retriever lay drooling on a black, icy patch of pavement. His collar and leather lead were hooked to a tree. I gave him a friendly sniff, a cheerful bark, arched my rump and lowered my shoulders. He wouldn't play. Resorting to straightforward conversation, I said, "Have you ever raced past a woodchuck just to hear his teeth clatter?"

"Gimme those bones or I'll give you a beating you won't survive," the swine-of-a-canine thunder-growled.

"Get lost flea farm," I said. "I'm not afraid of you." I stepped backwards. "I've had my tail caught in a crack before," I called over my shoulder as I spun and took off at a full gallop, "not tied to a tree. You can't catch me." By the time I reached Elizabeth, she was walking down our driveway. I was breathing hard. I skidded to a stop.

"Herbie honey, come here." Elizabeth rubbed her hands over my ribs. "You are out of breath because you're overweight." She held my head between her hands, making it impossible for me to check for the approach of the retriever. "If you carried these heavy books in your backpack every day when we walk you could lose some of that belly fat. Here, let me fix that suspender so you won't drag your bundle." She hummed as she worked, and then stood and pulled her car keys from her pocket. "Want to go to the bank with me?"

Of course I would. I got my best sleep riding in her car. Besides, being with Elizabeth was always an adventure. In no time we were in Jackson at her bank.

"Come on, sweet pea. Keep me company while we wait our turn for the ATM." As we stood in line behind a man with heavy black eyebrows, she said, "We need flour and milk and sugar and chocolate pudding." The line moved slower than it takes caterpillar larva to become a butterfly. "I'd better buy potatoes and onions and sour cream and a cake mix." Elizabeth used her grocery list to pass time while she was waiting like I used my nut list. "Herbie, you're out of milk bones."

I nodded agreement. When it was almost our turn at the ATM, the man in front of us inserted cards into the slot in the wall, and green papers came out of an opening. I couldn't take my eyes off his arms. They were covered in dark fur too, like a Labrador retriever's coat. I wondered if he might be of mixed breed, part dog and part man. He collected the papers and stepped away as Elizabeth inserted her only plastic card.

Before her green papers emerged from the slot, sirens screamed. Elizabeth crouched next to me. Cars with flashing lights surrounded the bank. Men jumped from the cars. Crows perched on streetlights flew away. The scent of fear swept through the crowd. Men rushed the building with guns drawn. I smelled shoe polish as they walked among us.

People in the ATM line panicked. Some ran for cover. Others banged into one another trying to get away before any shooting started. Women screamed and reached for the sky where the crows were circling. Some children rolled into balls on the sidewalk next to their sprawling mothers. An old person squatted with her hands above her head and walked like a duck.

Elizabeth was crushed against the building by the man who was in line in front of us. Before I could reach her, I was jerked aside and thrown to the ground by my backpack. I landed on my side with someone's knee pushing against my ribs. I didn't try to move until the person got off and disappeared in the confusion.

A gunshot echoed against the building. Movement stopped. I smelled gun powder and heard a child whimpering. After a long silence, the men walked among us and announced that the man they had been looking for had escaped. They apologized for any inconvenience and told us to have a nice day.

I was untangling from the mass when the sweet scent of relief rose like a cloud from the disarray replacing the acrid scent of fear. I stood to adjust the weight of my backpack. I located Elizabeth, sniffed her arms and legs, and licked her ears.

"I'm okay, Herbie. Let's get out of here and go shopping. But first I need some cash." Elizabeth stood, straightened her skirt and pushed buttons on the machine. Green papers slid from the slot. "It won't take me long at the store." She flashed papers at me before she stuck them in her purse. "I'll trade these for food and then we can go home."

It wasn't long before we were home, Elizabeth was unloading plastic grocery sacks from the hatchback, and we discovered the white-haired lady banging on our front door. She was about to accuse me of stealing her soup bones.

* * *

Although this woman looks like she may have seen ninety seasons, she can pound with the strength of a bull mastiff. She stops when she sees Elizabeth emerge from the hatchback, arms wrapped around the groceries.

"I'm missing twenty pounds of soup bones," she shouts at her. "They were cooling on my porch bench." Her booming voice is pitched high and tickles the insides of my ears as I jump from the car. "During all the years I have lived on this lake," she screeches, "I have never locked a door."

I am shaking the sound from my ears when Bob appears from inside the cottage. "What's going on out here? A horrible squeal woke me from a sound sleep." He takes the plastic bags from Elizabeth.

"I purchased a bundle of bones from the meat market," the woman explains as she looks towards Elizabeth now standing behind Bob.

"Who are you?" says Bob to the woman.

"I browned them in my oven and put them on my porch bench to cool." She glances at Bob, and then stretches her neck to speak to Elizabeth.

"It is you!" Bob shouts. "You are the one with the earth-shattering screech." He steps towards her and says, "Lady, I come home from work with a headache. I lay down to take a nap and what do I hear? Waves lapping against my shore? No. Birds chirping outside my window? No. I hear some old mare screaming at 60 decibels. What the devil are you baying about?"

"Bob, take it easy. Mrs. Howard is missing her soup bones."

"I would rather talk with your wife, sir." Mrs. Howard smiles at Bob and addresses Elizabeth. "When I next looked, the braising pan was empty."

"My head is throbbing and you're concerned about bones?" Bob growls. "Elizabeth, you deal with her, but if I find your mud-magnet is involved he's going to the dog pound." Bob spins, and slams the door leaving me, Hattie and Mrs. Howard standing outside, in silence.

The woman looks down at me with round eyes. I can read her thoughts. I explain to her in a long, low whine that Elizabeth has an elevated level of tolerance for eccentricity, unseemly personal habits, and lack of pedigree perfection. She pays no attention to members of her family who could never blend into civilized society.

Mrs. Howard's frown disappears and is replaced by a knowing look. She actually smiles at me, like she understands.

"I found huge paw prints in the snow near my bench," she whispers to Elizabeth. "I am investigating every large dog in this neighborhood." She points at me. "Why is your dog howling? I hope he doesn't wake your husband."

Elizabeth signs for me to stop with eyes as hard as stones. "Herbie loves singing that song," she tells the woman. "Come inside, Mrs. Howard. I bet you could use a cup of tea." Elizabeth's eyes grow dark and turn on me as Mrs. Howard steps inside the front door. "You don't need help getting into trouble, do you?"

That's right. Blame the dog. I know what's next unless I move fast. I race to Elizabeth's garden and bury the soup bones, the backpack and the books…all in one deep hole. As I disguise the soil intrusion with piles of dead leaves I smile inside my cheek. Elizabeth won't think of looking here until next spring when her tulips bloom.

I'm resting under the pin oak in the bright sunlight trying to comprehend the advance workings of Elizabeth's mind when she steps outside and surprises me. She takes my head between her hands, stares into my eyes and says, "Herbie, you must not steal." She looks past my eyes with such intensity I'm sure she can see clear through to my poop chute. "Do you understand me?"

"That would be an emphatic yes," I whine. This woman knows everything.

"Mrs. Hartman, thanks for the tea." Mrs. Howard says stepping outside. "I'm sorry to have bothered you."

Just then trouble pulls into our driveway. I can hear the man talk into his hand from inside his car. "I'm at the Hartman residence and can see the dog." A tall man steps from his vehicle. He approaches the women who are oblivious to his presence. I dash over to smell his crotch.

He's a sexually active male who eats red meat and is in a pleasant mood today. His last meal was…ice cream…chocolate ice cream. I smell gun powder and shoe polish. He pets my head. "Nice dog," he says but I sense he doesn't mean it. How could he know that? He just met me.

When Elizabeth sees the man she calls me to her and gives me the hand command for sit and stay. She and the man talk quietly. She glances around the yard and then throws up her hands like something is lost. He gives her a small piece of paper, they shake hands, and he drives away.

I can tell Elizabeth is nervous as Mrs. Howard and she saunter up the driveway because she removes her sweater and wipes her forehead with the back of her hand. Mrs. Howard fans herself with her braising pan.

"I'm sorry to have bothered you when you're in trouble with the police. It's just that I promised to make my friend a pot of soup…he lost his teeth and…"

"How awful. Was he in an accident?" Elizabeth says.

"No, it was a fight. He lost them in the lake while he was bringing in a walleye."

"That's funny, Mrs. Howard." Elizabeth chuckles. "I'm sorry about your soup bones. I'll notify you if I track them down." She turns her head toward mine and whispers, "I should be able to find them if the snow keeps melting like it has all morning. Herbie, I know you like to dig holes. Sometimes you aren't as smart as you think you are."

Elizabeth crosses and uncrosses her fingers, wiggling them like scissors as she and Mrs. Howard linger by the roadside. The old lady leaves for home carrying her braising pan and a plate of Elizabeth's oatmeal cookies.

I am not smiling as my guardian hooks on my leash. I am not cracking wise as we follow Mrs. Howard up the sunset road toward her house. And I'm certainly not happy to see the damage to the snow the sun has made. I keep my head down, and my eyes trained on the road as we walk. Elizabeth's holds her chin up, her eyes lapping up the landscape, looking this way and that way, until she locates a certain hickory nut tree.

"Aha!" is all she says.

I'm still not smiling, eating cookies or lingering anywhere. I am tethered to this pin oak in my own yard for stealing bones, but I'm suffering even more from the picture inside my head…the neighborhood dogs loitering in the afternoon sunshine, devouring my stolen *cache* before Elizabeth discovers the rest. The thought makes me want to run in circles. Here I am, boneless, feeling cheated by the degrees, smarting because I didn't get the bones and feeling guilty because I did. A low howl sprouts from my throat which rises in pitch and volume until I can be heard across the lake. By nightfall my voice is raw and crusty.

Bob appears outside with his hands on his hips, a deep frown splitting his forehead. Elizabeth joins him and says, "Looks like another big storm brewing." Bob looks like he is full of thunder and lightning. "Will you roll the trash can inside the carport before it hits?" she says.

"Sure, sure." He's staring at me like the dog catcher about to throw his net. I sense he cares more about thrashing me than moving trash. "Stop the howling Herbie or I'll duct tape your mouth shut."

"Bob, I heard you," says Elizabeth, "and that is a terrible thing to say to this defenseless little puppy I bought for your birthday. What if he understands you? You could frighten him. We are all the family he has. Lighten up."

"Okay. Okay," he says, and pivots towards me and winks. I can see his fingers crossed behind his back. "I'm so sorry, Herbie. Please stop the howling." When Elizabeth walks inside Bob leans over and in a threatening whisper says, "If that noise resumes, I will tie your tongue into a knot, and then duct tape your mouth shut."

"You can't scare me you poison toad," I snarl in a whisper, coming into my maleness. "You're just an annoying male know-it-all." I growl slightly less softly. "You probably think you are the smartest frog in the forest," I whine and wiggle my bottom. "So, you think you're so smart," I mouth soundlessly while looking directly at the alpha to show aggression. "Are you smarter than the firefly that lights the inside of my mouth to avoid getting bitten?" As soon as the last sound escapes my throat I hurdle around the corner and hide under the forsythia bush.

SEVEN

When the wind changes, I catch their scent. I have been guarding Elizabeth as she strips vegetables from her autumn garden. Calle and a large German shepherd have been watching from the next yard since shortly before the sun was highest and hottest.

"These are the last of the potatoes and carrots," Elizabeth says. "Herbie, move off those onions or your coat will smell bad."

I lay on my stomach and watch her pull plants from the garden one by one…the dead tomato plants, stringy squash vines, a large leafed zucchini skeleton and a mound of dried carrot tops. She works slowly and methodically. She strips the leaves, breaks the stalks and stuffs them into compost bins.

There is nothing more twitch-inducing than waiting for something to happen. It is impossible to focus on Elizabeth while I am under surveillance. Calle and her friend follow our movements with interest.

"Herbie. Pay attention," Elizabeth says.

I check behind me, nothing but sunshine. Without glancing at them I can sense the dogs are still watching.

"You have the attention span of an infant." Elizabeth holds her finger in front of my nose. She lifts her hand to her face so my gaze will follow to her eyes. "I want you to keep the deer away…and the rabbits, and the opossum and the raccoons. I'm counting on you to scare them away before they eat the tulip bulbs I just planted."

With Elizabeth beside me I tongue my paws clean, scan my surroundings for poachers, and lick my chest hair white. The two dogs in the next yard stare at us while we work.

Elizabeth returns to the kitchen door and calls out. "Herbie! I forgot to mention squirrels. I don't want them burying their black walnuts in my garden." As she enters the cottage I overhear her say, "I know he's not a stupid dog, although sometimes he acts like one." When I hear the door slam shut my mind drifts.

Pippin was my alpha at Ken-Bear's kennel. He was my birth-father. I had to bear his calling me Number Four in my litter until I could earn a more dignified and appropriate name, like his: Champion Ken-Bear's N Wigglebottom's Pippin. I scratch my ear as I remember his sternness.

"Stop whining Number Four and get your poop in a pile! Look at me when I'm barking. Never forget your genes are from champion Old English sheepdog stock. We are bred to protect sheep from wolves, and to kill predators if necessary.

Number Four, sit still! Stop wiggling!" He often gave me the stink eye. "You will be strong and have a productive career if you can manage to keep your coat free from burdocks. Now run along and try to keep the noise down."

My folks rarely stayed home after I was weaned. They spent most of their time traveling the show circuit. I have no memory of being lonely. Four kittens had been born the same day as the other five puppies in my litter. A big knot forms in my throat when I think of them. We all played in one big whelping pen until one by one they were adopted, each one picked but two kittens and me. I rather enjoyed being the last puppy chosen, languishing in my parents kennel with no responsibilities. They slathered me with attention when they were home. I yearn for the warmth of that birth pack.

That happiness ended when Elizabeth whisked me away to this lake, this neighborhood, this yard and this garden. I am bone tired, mildly confused and occasionally dizzy. I begin to howl at the bottom of the scale, move up past the middle and pitch into the higher ranges of dog desolation. I feel small and gloomy under this sun. I wonder if dogs live on the stars. I wonder if the Irish setter and that German shepherd are the only other dogs in this lake kingdom. While I howl questions to the day-sun, hungry clouds gnaw the sunshine away and are replaced by a featherishly purple dusk. The only answer to come my way is from the aging dog next door.

The German shepherd had crawled away while I was singing. Calle stayed and heard it all. She may have been too tired to move. She's old. Anyone can see that at one time this canine had been a beauty.

The white blaze on her face highlights what still is a spectacular red coat except for the gray around her muzzle. Her boots are still white. The rest of her medium-long, soft coat has grayed into a dull, lifeless tan. When she moves she humps her back like she hurts from inside. The old girl sits on her side of the braided wire fence, sighing as she settles on the sod. She speaks to me quietly without making eye contact. Passing her paw along the entire vault of the sky, she begins where the sun rises and ends where the sun sets. She signs that for far too many moons she has been listening to my sorrows and fears.

"I have told you before, being a sun-struck dog is not good for your reputation," Calle says. "Herbie, if you are heard sobbing with day terrors, some may think you are a coward." She pauses to scratch her ear and catch a fly in her mouth, chew and swallow it. "It is only natural to feel bad, Herbie, but you must walk bravely and weep inside your cheek."

I can't look in Calle's direction. When I paw my eyes to hold back the tears I catch a whiff of my coat. It smells like stupid. My muzzle drops until my nose rubs the grass. "I can't help crying," I tell her. "I lack courage. I have defects. It's not in me to walk like I'm brave. My sire shuffles like a bear… like his sire shuffled before him. You better change my name to Runs Scared Like A Rabbit."

"Ken-Bear's kennel no longer exists as home for you. It is time to move on, but move with honor." She pauses. "Or, you can be a quitter and a coward and live your life in a dark doghouse, alone and afraid." Like smoke, Red Dog is gone.

I coil around on the ground to have a good think. I do want to live up to the greatness of my name, yet don't have a clue how…can't imagine what a channel feels like…am uncertain how to determine which is the right channel if and when I do locate one. I shake hair from my eyes so I can see, stand and stretch my back. I wonder if I should believe this wolf that talks inside my head. I wonder why that dark stranger sits in his car on our road all day. I wonder why my foot hurts. I find Bob's baseball glove on the patio table. I wonder if it will float as long as his cap did.

EIGHT

Calle is gone from my yard when the large German shepherd arrives. He circles me, stops, turns, then reverses his ring. His ears stand upright pricked to a point, his head is cocked to one side like he's wondering how a dead dog can snore. I watch his circling through the slits in my eyes and hold back a grin. It will be comical if the big dog grows dizzy and falls over.

The grin evaporates as I remember a dream I had about Beau's death. I can't recall the details, but he does get dizzy and falls. A shiver goes from my tail hole to my withers. Stop dreaming, I tell myself. This dog is too grand for laughter. It will be tragic when he falls.

The shepherd's neck hangs over my body like a tree limb. A black mist is steaming from his coat. His front feet knead the ground. I wonder if he is standing on an anthill and glance under his belly to have a look. I lay motionless as he sniffs my rump in greeting. He swings around, inhales scents from my head and then around my belly and bung hole again.

The big dog doesn't carry an aggressive scent, yet I can't help but fidget when he pokes his snout under my chest. I pull a burdock from my paw while his muzzle moves over my belly. I summon all my courage to look up as the shepherd addresses me. Instinct reminds me direct eye contact is a sign of aggression, so I look over his head.

"Vhich end bites?" He directs his voice to my butt and nestles his snot locker between my testicles. "Hello male dog with long hair on both ends." He walks around me to sniff what he thinks is my nose. His voice holds sternness, a hard-bitten quality that makes me want to pay attention. I understand the question and shake back strands of hair covering my face.

His tail wags. "Vhat a surprise! Here are brown eyes at this end." His eyeballs become slits and his smooth black lips pull tight and up at the corners. "And you have a big nose, black and capricious. Allow me to introduce myself. I am Beau, from the Schmidt family. I live on the road that leads to the sunsets. Vhat do they call this end of you?"

I stand. It's my turn to investigate. I move my nose into the short coarse hair around Beau's nose. His scent is one of dominance with hints of a pleasant temperament. I move behind him to sniff his anal scent glands. This dog is male, adult and is bathed regularly. His last meal was…yes, dry kibble with a hint of dead squirrel. I wonder if he ate my former friend Lazy on the north wind road. I'm afraid to ask.

"They call me Ken-Bear's Herbie the Love Bug," I say. "My pack name is Hartman. Oh, and Calle just gave me another name."

"You are Valks Like a Bear. I already know."

My mouth gapes open in surprise.

"Ya. I am hearing about you. My duty in this neighborhood is to velcome new dogs and to inform them of the rules." The German shepherd's coat is brushed smooth and shining on top, his ears are erect and creamy white. "It is verboten to vaste your urine in one spot," he says. "You must never pass a tree, bush or rock near the roadway vithout marking it vith your news." His gray legs are booted with identical black paws and tipped with neatly clipped toenails. "It is forbidden for male dogs to squat. You must learn to lift your leg to do your business." He has champion lines, strong shoulders, beautifully chiseled facial features, and a long tail arching around to a perfect curve over his back. "It is against our laws to be caught on another dog's property vithout permission. Chasing deer is off limits." The big dog's effect is one of confidence, a top dog in complete control. "Digging holes in rose gardens is not appreciated. Most important, vhen vinter comes, do not lick the yellow snow. Versteh'?"

I yawn in agreement to release my stress, but am convinced a dog who thinks another dog should think like he does is out of his mind. My muscles lose their tightness during the next yawn and yawn extension. By the time I yawn again my ears have flopped forward covering my eyes and nose.

"If you fall asleep no one vill see you," he grins. "Very vell then, you look different but you are welcome to live among us." The big dog's silvery-gray hair glistens from the light of the yard pole. He spins around, plants his paws and looks back to see if I'm watching. When he strides away, his nails click a perfect rhythm on the hard pavement.

And that is how I met Beau Schmidt.

NINE

Crisp crimson leaves have fallen from the maples long ago and lay hidden beneath the winter white. It's the cold season. I am padding over the softness scanning for a patch of green grass soft enough to chew when I sense something is wrong… different…missing. Elizabeth refers to this flat prairie of water as "that dangerous lake that you must never walk across."

A malfunction in the air lures me, fuels my curiosity. I think at first the tension I sense is the lack of movement in the water. I haven't heard the wind blowing water into waves for days. I tap the surface to break it like Elizabeth showed me on my water dish. Nothing. I repeat the tap. This water will not shatter. The surface is smooth on my paws, cold, hard and slick. I inch out. My back legs skid. My front legs slip. I land on my belly. My chin knocks hard and snaps my teeth shut.

That was when it happened. A rumble roared along the newly formed lake ice, a twirling rip that rattled towards me, bearing down the brittle surface like a garbage truck, coming, arriving, and then moving on. Calle warned me this would happen. She said it would be the ice arguing with the sun's early morning rays about what was right today and what was wrong. I was supposed to listen when nature spoke.

While attempting to stand I notice the rhythmic clip of sharp hooves and see an animal chasing a white tailed deer down the shoreline and out onto the lake. The predator's paws thud and pulse so heavily, I can feel the surface shudder beneath me. From where I'm sprawled it looks like a dog, but it could be a coyote. That deer is definitely a buck. I can see his antlers.

The marauder snaps at the white tail's heels. It circles and barks, assaulting an animal triple its size. The buck pivots and strikes with his hoof-slicing forefeet, battling back his attacker. The assassin is down, knocked back by the buck's defensive maneuver and slides across the ice. The brute, stumbles to his feet and forges forward with one gimpy leg to resume its offense strike. The buck twists. It turns and staves off the beast's third offensive.

When I squint I see the predator is a wolf, a gray wolf with a limp. The buck slips and skids on the slick surface and sinks to his knees. The sleek deer struggles upright, his muscles wet and rippling in the sunlight. He barks a counter threat at the wolf. He is ready to resume the fight, but doesn't seem to be aware of an even greater danger that threatens from below: a whirling, zigzagging, splitting noise.

The wolf knows. The wolf responds. I see him stop his circling, crouch, and inch towards shore. The gray stops moving, and flattens his body until the ice stops speaking. Edging backwards, he crawls across the ice and watches nature's cruelty from the safety of the shore.

The crack comes before the plunge. The splash comes before the thrashing legs. This buck is on the underside of his luck.

The wolf stares at the struggle, and unhurried, he turns and lopes into the forest, his lame leg barely touching the ground. He leaves the stag for the lake to take.

I must sound an alarm, but realize I can't while I'm standing on a lake forbidden to me. I scratch my ear and ponder if I should bark for help and face Elizabeth's wrath, or race to get help for the buck and be discovered. Indecision makes me itch. Itching eventually gets me to the right channel.

A howl erupts from my throat. The sound stretches across the lake, bounces off rocks, passes rabbits covering their ears and alerts crows circling above. I skid towards home howling for Elizabeth.

"What?" Elizabeth cracks open the door as she tucks her shirt into her jeans. "Herbie, what did I tell you about…"

My barking accelerates. I run in circles and point my muzzle towards the frozen lake. Puzzlement fills her eyes until she sees the commotion. Elizabeth steps into her boots, grabs her parka and stomps along the deep shoreline snow towards the opening in the ice. She tosses a "Good dog, Herbie" over one shoulder, and waves to a human figure moving on the frozen lake ahead. "What can I do?" No answer. She staggers along the seawalls and repeats her offer. This time she shouts. "Sylvia, I want to help!"

I squint to assess the situation from where I tramp beside my guardian. I see a person pushing a canoe onto the ice. The buck is splashing in open water, his flailing front feet catch a hold on a chunk of ice. He grips the edge with black tipped hooves and lifts his great neck. Steam streams clouds from his snout into the cold air.

The buck struggles, pulling himself up on the ice with his strong forefeet. He claws the slick surface with his sharp back hooves until he is lying flat and still on the lake's icy surface. I can see his sides heaving with heavy breathing before he tries to stand. A foot slips. His bulk slams down hard on a knee and the thin surface collapses beneath him. The poor beast plunges back into the frigid pit, hitting his head on a slice of ice before slipping under.

I recognize the female inside the watercraft as Elizabeth's friend…the one who pulls my ears then gives me treats.

"I sure hope he's able to find the hole he breached. It's his sole escape route from under that ice sheet," she calls to Elizabeth. With one leg outside the craft propelling the canoe, she heads towards the opening in the ice and reaches it just as the stag surfaces, thrashing his legs and gasping.

"Sylvia!" Elizabeth shouts. "I'm coming out to help."

"Use the ladder leaning on the lodge," Sylvia shouts.

"Herbie, stay!" Elizabeth's tone is brimming with authority. She flattens one hand in front of my face and snatches a ski rope with the other. She ties one end to the ladder, and while lying on her stomach propels it out over the ice behind the deer. "This ice won't hold much," she tells Sylvia.

The stag is clutching the edge at a jagged breaking point.

"Hurry," Sylvia shouts. "Loop the rope around his neck."

Elizabeth whirls the rope over her head and throws. The loop encircles the buck's neck on the first try. She pulls it tight. "Lucky break."

"Will you look at that cowgirl skill," Sylvia laughs. "Now throw the skier's grip to me?"

The wooden handle circles wider and higher in the air as Elizabeth whirls the rope. She lets go and hits the side of Sylvia's canoe.

"Nice," Sylvia says grasping the wood. "Now back away... further…pull the rope taunt…move toward shore where the water is shallow."

I can hear the ice crack from where I watch on shore.

"It isn't thick enough for both of us," Sylvia says. "Move away from me. Faster!"

I see Elizabeth moving stomach-flat, balancing on the ladder, propelling herself toward shore using her arms and legs like oars on a fishing boat. The rope trails the ladder over the ice.

"Hold on!" I bark over the ice to the distressed animal. I see a hoof slip. The buck is losing his grip, or giving up. "Don't do it. Don't let go," I warn him. "There's a wolf down there, too. That one will be chasing you forever." I bark louder as the buck sinks deeper. "You're just having a bad day. Don't lose your grip. Trust me. That wolf in the underwater will drive you crazy in the head."

"Elizabeth, he's tiring. We may lose him," Sylvia shouts. "Keep that rope taut."

"Watch it, you're too…" Elizabeth screams as the ice cracks under Sylvia's canoe. Open water proves a slick path for the stern to plunge, dipping the craft beneath the black surface and just missing the buck. Movement slows. The center of the canoe is caught. The narrow vessel jerks to a stop at a sharp angle. Sylvia loses her grip, slips, and skids toward the lower end of the canoe, the end that is underwater. I hear a thud. The vessel is wedged in the crevice.

"Sylvia!" Elizabeth yells and jerks the line wrapped around the buck's neck.

Sylvia doesn't answer.

Elizabeth pulls the rope encircling the buck's head, the same rope that leads to Sylvia's canoe. Elizabeth's tug gets the buck's attention, but it is his instinct that jolts him up onto the ice and to his feet. It is pure desire that carries him away from the weakening edge. Once he is safe he collapses in a pile.

"Save the buck!" Sylvia shouts from inside the sinking canoe. "I'm stable."

Another yank on the rope drags the buck forward, raking his belly across ice crusted snow. Elizabeth pulls the rope hand over hand. The buck slides forward, his neck twists at an awkward angle. A single line of crimson marks the ice behind his body. Elizabeth strains and drags the heavy creature toward shore. The buck's stock-still legs straggle, dangling behind his skidding bulk.

As Elizabeth moves I hear the ice crack, rending the air with sharp, threatening snaps. The buck slides over the splintering surface. He has nothing left: no vigor to stand and run and no energy to avoid crevices opening in the ice to his left and behind.

Elizabeth keeps the rope pressure constant as she digs into the snow covered ice, step by step. She slides the splayed buck's body over the creaking lake and as close to shore as snow banks allow.

Trailing the deer is the canoe. Elizabeth unwinds the rope from the buck's neck and hand pulls the canoe into shore. Sylvia is lying on her stomach in the bottom, still holding the skier's wooden handle. She gets to her knees and climbs out.

51

"Close one," Sylvia coughs. They both laugh.

I bark and head towards the animal lying on the ice. He's shivering. I lick his shoulder and listen. I can barely hear his heartbeat.

"Herbie, come! I don't trust this ice to hold us all." Elizabeth belly-crawls toward the stag, rearranges his legs beneath him and pulls a front leg gently onto the soft snow near shore.

Sylvia is back on the ice, this time pushing the buck from behind. "Be careful, Elizabeth. Front hooves can be lethal. Deer use them for protection."

A crowd of neighbors have gathered on the beach. Some are carrying blankets, others beach towels. They take turns rubbing the stag's freezing frame.

"He's still breathing," says a bull-strong female who lives nearby. She is almost square with a low center of gravity. I smell her crotch: adult female; last meal was pig; mood is belligerent. I have identified her scent once before during my walk. It was the last time the moon was full and the smell of steaming hot soup slid from her kitchen window.

"He'll be okay. Let's get him warm and work the cramps from his back legs," the burly one rumbles. "Shouldn't cause trouble…too tired to move." Her tone is so low and rugged it makes the ground shiver when she speaks. I sense she can be mean. "Sylvia, you're wet. Get inside by the fire before you get frostbite!.."

"I saw a dog chase that deer on the ice," says a small boy with a squeak of a voice. I know he is too young to have a serious scent so I pass on sniffing his crotch.

"That was no dog," says the hefty female. "That was a wolf."

"Can't be a wolf," says an older man, a stranger. "There are no wolves this far south of Isle Royale. They were chased off down here fifty years ago."

"It was a coyote," a gravelly sound comes from the strapping woman's throat. "Damn coyote was smarter than this here buck…ran off the ice when it first began to crack. You," the woman orders an onlooker. "Massage his leg from over here."

Neighbors banter about this and that while taking turns rubbing the exhausted stag. They stroke his leg muscles until his joints bend, then cover him with blankets. The group breaks up to accept an invitation for mugs of hot cocoa inside a nearby lodge.

While they are inside, I creep closer to have a look. The buck has a deep gash on one side of his head. The bleeding is stopped and a bloody scab is forming. His eyes move as I circle him; his black pupils grow large. Smelling his fear, I lick his nose to calm him and lay with my warmth along his spine. "Some days are like this…living below luck level. Tomorrow will be better." I wrap my hind leg over his. "Did you cut your face on the ice?" I say after a time.

"Wolf…snagged…" the buck whispers in one short, declining, breath.

"Don't talk. Rest," I say. Sometime later I hear a door drag open, the buzz of conversation and feel a tremor after the sturdy woman's laugh. The sound of familiar voices sails along the air. I hear Sylvia with Elizabeth. She's wearing different clothes. I smell chocolate. A door bangs shut.

"What would I have done if you had fallen in?" Elizabeth says to Sylvia.

"Good question. In case we have another ice emergency we should have a plan. You could push the ladder across the hole. Then I could grab a rung and pull myself out. Or you could skid out atop the ladder and pull me out."

"That canoe was a brilliant idea," Elizabeth says. "It distributed your weight."

"If you had a rope, you could throw one end to me," Sylvia says. "I know a man who always carries a screwdriver in his pocket when he's out on the ice. He used it once to pull himself out. The trick is to stay calm and think." Sylvia chuckles. She points. "Will you look at that? Herbie has made a new friend. I didn't know deer and dogs got along."

I feel the stag's spine twitch and tumble away. The big buck folds his legs under his belly, rolls upright and stands. He is worn-down, and banged-up. His knees wobble. His torso weaves. He shakes loose the blankets that hang from his back, stumbles across the sunset road and bounds into the woods. A blink later I see him loping across the cornfield, his white tail bobbing in the distance. He seems unhurried as he vanishes into a willow swale.

The empty bowl of night envelopes us all on the short walk home. Drained, I am asleep before I finish my kibble.

"Elizabeth, will you look at that?" I hear Bob say.

"Keep your voice down. You'll scare the pup."

"The mutt is sleeping with his head in his food bowl," Bob says. "Elizabeth, would they have sold you a smart dog for the same price you paid for this one?"

"Come out from under the table, honey," Elizabeth whispers to me when Bob has gone to bed. "Don't feel bad. It's hard for Bob to show his love. It's just the way he is, but he's a good man, very smart, and he takes good care of us."

Wrong, Elizabeth. He's dull…so dull he causes dullness in others. If you thinks he's smart, let him try using his intellect on that lake wolf. Just have him try ordering that lake-monster around and see what happens.

TEN

A foreign scent floats over my nose as I stretch and groan and bleep sleep from my eyes. I lift my nose to determine its source and notice Beau, the German shepherd, standing at the entrance of my kingdom. He must be waiting for my invitation to enter. I smile, pleased with a visit from such a prominent neighbor.

"It has come to our attention, Valks Like a Bear, that you are not marking trees," Beau says as he lumbers across my lawn. "You are squatting like a girl." He stops next to me and averts his eyes so he will not appear aggressive.

I don't relish being spied upon when I sleep and by all rights should run this dog out by his tail, but I do want him to like me. Besides, Beau Schmidt is a respected member of our neighborhood, so I must honor the spirit of the Bear and use my manners. I take a breath to rest my thoughts. I don't know how to handle this situation, so I fake a glance around my yard so he'll think I'm expecting someone important.

Beau must have sensed my discomfort. "Calle asked me to vatch your progress. She needs to be certain you are a dog who vants to learn."

I am bewildered why hitting a tree with my pee is so important to the neighborhood canines. I shrug, pleased with myself for playing down a skill such a distinguished dog says is so vital and drop the fake boundaries I had set.

"It is impossible for any dog to read a message left by your mark," Beau says. "Ve are unable to smell your sex, age, mood, or last meal after you pass by. Vatch as I demonstrate balance and the angle of the leg." Beau walks to the red cedar, cocks his back leg to a vertical position and aims his urine four feet up where the deer have been chewing the bark. "Versteh?' You vill try now."

I walk over, lift my leg and let go. "Like this?"

"Nein. You vill vatch me again. Notice how my back leg points straight up?" he says and marks the tree even higher. "You vill try that angle."

I am nervous and self-conscious that an act as natural as a pee can be so complex or take such athletic prowess. I think I understand the moves, but what I don't know is what else I don't know about where or how you pee or poop and why and when you sneeze and howl. "Thanks for the demonstration," I say, dismissing Beau with a nod and stepping towards the cottage.

"You are velcome. You vill do it again."

Try as hard as I can, my rear leg will not point toward the sky. I don't think I'm hinged right for a vertical pee. I hit the back of my front leg each time I try. My pristine white leg hair is now spotted yellow and smells of urine.

Beau shifts his weight from one foot to another as he watches. I can see he is not a patient dog. He stands, marks the tree again, and says, "You vill take your turn?"

I am intent on pleasing my new friend. I will myself to hit that tree, aim and let go. This time I miss my leg, but hit the grass not far from where Beau stands.

The big dog backs up a step, patiently points his leg and pees up the tree. "Now you," he instructs.

During this next blast Beau steps back quickly but not quickly enough. I hit his leg. "I'm sorry, Beau. I wouldn't dream of…didn't mean to…" I'm finding this a daunting task.

"Again! Again!" Beau shakes the urine from his leg. "You vill try one more time to be sure. You don't vant to shame the neighborhood. Good. Ya, this is much better, but you need to practice."

Beau's patience must be waning or maybe he's just out of urine because he asks if anyone has taught me how to leave a time message.

"No," I shudder, trying to imagine the physical prowess a clock requires.

"You vill pay attention." Beau's tone has become stern. "You vill only hear this once." The German shepherd takes a deep breath and frowns. "First, draw a round sun on the ground vith your paw." He demonstrates and urges me to finish the circle. "Push a stick straight up in the middle."

I find a stick in Elizabeth's garden and give it to him.

"Now, draw a line like mine tracing the shadow of the stick. That line tells your friend vhere the sun vas sending its shadow vhen you left home." He noses a spot of sun in the sand and then paws where the shadow lay that is cast by the stick. "Any guest can compare the point vhen you left vith the point the shadow hits vhen they arrived. The difference between these two points vill determine how long it has been since you left your first mark. Do you understand, numbskull?" Beau looks straight into my eyes.

I see a smudge of dirt on his nose. "Why, y-y-yes I do," I say. I am lying because I'm embarrassed that I don't get it. "That is clever, Beau. Was the sun dial your invention?" I try to flatter the single-minded shepherd to interrupt his interrogation.

"Nein," Beau says. His face reflects amusement. "An ordinary sun dial like this has been used by animals and the

Potavatomi for many vinters. So, Valks Like a Bear, has the volf taught you any legends yet?"

"He told me some and Calle told me some. Does the wolf talk to you, too?" An unexpected yawn unhinges my jaw. I attempt to stifle it with my paw and accidentally make the sign our conversation is over.

Beau ignores the sign. He must be on a mission. "No one hears the volf but Calle sometimes, and now you. Calle tells the legends to everybody, vell at least she used to. She has forgotten so many. Her job is to remember everything. She's old. She used to know vhere all the bones vere buried. She is Keeper of the Legends."

Since the big dog is so intent on infusing me with knowledge, I ask a question I've been wondering about since I was small. "Beau, is it absolutely necessary for a dog to have a tail?"

"Nein." Beau answers without smiling and returns to his reserve of questions. He is like a hunter aching to use the contents of his loaded quiver. "Do you know how to bury a bone so no other animal can find it?"

"Yes." I say, but I don't. I'm lying, again.

"Do you know how to bark messages across the lake?"

"Yes, yes I do." I say. I wish he would go home. I'm uneasy because I don't want Beau to think I know so little. "Thank you for your help. Now, please excuse me, I need to go count the rocks in the seawall." I fib again. Turning, I squeeze my eyes tight, hating my need to lie, but despising my ignorance even more. I vow to learn everything worth knowing before I die. I vow to start with the next sun.

Beau stops in mid-stride on his way out of my yard. "Valks Like a Bear, always remember this: Do not corner something that you know is meaner than you."

"Right." I scratch my ear.

ELEVEN

A thorn bites my foot as I'm exploring Elizabeth's rose garden a few suns later. I yelp, then struggle with the pricker, chew and pull at it attempting to find a channel, a new way to get rid of the barb and the pain. Blood drips, splattering the snow red. I bark at Bob who stands in his pajamas inside the door. I hold up a bloody paw. He gives me a frown and continues licking the melted marshmallow from his cocoa. This man's compassion is as bland as dry kibble.

Elizabeth is arguing with the old grump. I don't know why she wastes her time. He stops sipping long enough to pucker his lips into a pout. That's how the scum sucker wins arguments with her. He makes her laugh, then wheedles and whines until she agrees. I wonder about this man's behavior. All his meanness couldn't have happened overnight. He must have been polishing it for a long time. But, give him a biscuit and he will sit or roll over for anyone.

Elizabeth lets me inside as their banter continues. They have been arguing for weeks. I get no response from either of them while I limp around the cottage and leave bloody paw prints on Elizabeth's pristine wood floor. Being injured is a lonely business. I grab my leash from the floor and hop over to the door. They ignore me.

"Will you stop complaining?" Elizabeth says to Bob. "Without that puppy a little flame of faithfulness, a touch of tenderness will be terribly lacking in our lives. Herbie is an excellent guard dog. He won't let a stranger get close to me. Just this morning a jogger came up behind me. Herbie rushed between us, growled at the man until he sprinted away. I can't send him back. Come on, you must be pleased we have him by now."

I push my empty water dish toward them with my nose. They ignore me, so I limp under the table, lie down and listen.

"No, I'm not pleased. Don't let that mutt on my chair. And by the way, why didn't you put the bedspread on this morning?"

"I did. I always do."

"Did not."

"Did, and don't call him a mutt. Herbie may understand what you're saying. Remember what your mother said…you can't unsay a cruel word."

"Get real, that dog can't understand me. The monster better get useful around here for the amount of money I spend on his food. "He walks into the bedroom and gets back into bed. Soon the old marshmallow-licker's heavy breathing turns to sets of shuddering snorts, then to a deep rumble, like a truck rolling over heavy gravel.

After the sun fills the sky again he reappears in a topcoat and leaves the house in a huff. When I have finished chewing the cable television remote, the night in me pulls me back. I hear myself breathing deeply, and don't remember much after that until I'm startled awake.

"Herbie?" Elizabeth's manner changes as she brushes her teeth. She becomes all sweetness and white foaming goop beguiling me with perfumed words like "honeybunch" this, "sweet knees" that and "move your cute jelly belly out of the doorway a little faster, please." She acts delightful, like peanut butter, but has the scent of a dog biscuit soaked in sour milk. I sense trouble.

It's already too late when I remember I haven't seen her drinking her morning coffee. I scratch my ear as thunder cracks. Dark clouds are massing. The ground beneath me rumbles.

"Why aren't you wiggling and jumping in circles? We're going for a ride. You always like riding in the car." Elizabeth bends down, takes my head in her hands. "Look honey, it's just a routine office call."

I wiggle free.

"Herbie, come out of that closet!" She ties her shoes. With an ear-piercing shout she squeals, "Let's go. The doctor will give you a poke to test your blood for Lyme disease and heart worm." She holds up a wrapped specimen I expelled during our walk. "He wants to test this for worms." Her pitch moves into the annoying, dangerously high range as she pulls on her coat. "Herbie, come out from under that bed."

I smell a storm all right. I'm not fooled by scented words. I know worms sleep deep in compost and not in my dog scat. She has another agenda. Elizabeth's tone changes as she pops open the back gate of the station wagon. Her voice pitches down to the trenches of serious compliance.

"Herbie, get your butt into this car, now!"

I crawl from under the bed frame, creep toward the exit and push the screen door open with my nose. I don't know why I have to go. I'm a good dog…she tells me that every day. I eat that suffocating droll kibble she pours into my bowl. I relieve myself twice a day. In time, Elizabeth will learn it's too much trouble to take a dog like me to a veterinarian. I jump into the station wagon.

She talks all the while she's driving. She tells me how the dog doctor can control where fleas sink their fangs. She says it's like controlling whom dogs bite. I don't like where this conversation is going. As she chatters I watch trees flash by the window. All I want the doctor to fix is my bloody foot, and I expect a biscuit for that consideration.

Elizabeth resorts to coaxing me from the car with a treat because she can't reach my choke collar. Inside the waiting room I wait next to Elizabeth while she answers questions like…what is your home address…what is the home address of your former employer…has your dog ever bitten anyone… who played Lassie in films after Lassie retired? Why do they need to know all this weirdness? Elizabeth reads a magazine while I look around at the other animals waiting and wonder what dread disease will send them up behind the Milky Way.

She has no trouble dragging me into a treatment room that reeks of disinfectant while she has me on a choke chain. I exaggerate my limp on the way in to give the doctor a clue why I'm here.

"Mrs. Hartman, your sheep dog seems to be in perfect health," the veterinarian announces after prodding and poking and peeking and pummeling. He flashes Elizabeth a wide smile. "Any questions?"

"I have one," I growl. "I have a sore foot and I'm limping. Will someone let me know as soon as this doctor shows some intelligence?"

He ignores me.

"Don't growl at the doctor, Herbie," she says to me. "Doctor Hauschild, I do have a question," Elizabeth says to him. "Herbie will not let me touch his foot. Did you notice his limp?"

Good job, Elizabeth. At least you're observant, I whine.

"No, Mrs. Hartman. It would be a pronounced limp if something serious is wrong. His walk is normal. Just keep him at home and quiet for a few days."

Here's my home remedy for a limp, doctor. Send me home, I growl. Neither one of them pays a bit of attention to my suggestions.

"Please check him for open sores, broken nails or anything that might cause him pain," Elizabeth insists and holds my head so I don't turn toward him and sink my teeth into his flesh.

I tell you there's nothing wrong with me but the pain in my paw, I whimper, but the doctor seizes my foot and pulls it towards him. Don't touch me! I cry. I'm suddenly too warm. Let go of me! That hurts, I growl. I can't breathe from the pain. I choke. I cannot get away…cannot get loose…smells bad in here…too hot…have to fight. Want to flee. I can't catch my breath.

"Easy, boy," says the doctor.

Easy for you. It's not your foot. I yank, twist, and throw my weight this way and that. I jerk my foot, but the doctor's grip is firm. Disinfectant perfumes the room. It's overpowering. I feel like I might vomit. Drop my foot! I bark. Bad doctor!

"It's okay, Herbie," Elizabeth says in that patronizing tone she uses when she's lying. She pats my head. "Just relax, honey. Doctor Hauschild wants to help you." She strokes my hair flat to my face and nods to the veterinarian. "I think he's relaxing, doctor."

I hate the feel of my hair slicked flat to my face. I'm caught, trapped like that raccoon in the steel trap near our cottage. Will I have to chew my leg off to break free the way the raccoon did? If this doctor hurts me, I'll hurt him right back! I tip my muzzle for fresh air and smell soap…the stinky, germ-killing kind that can kill a bug, or make a bumblebee sneeze. "No soap," I whine. Adrenalin spreads inside me like venom from a bee sting. I am trapped and am struggling to breathe. With all my strength I wrench my foot forward.

"Mrs. Hartman, can you keep him from squirming so much?" Doctor Hauschild is puffing. "Hold your dog around his torso," he orders, reaching for a spray bottle.

I smell Elizabeth's perspiration as she holds my hindquarters. She smells sweet. The doctor smells of dirty socks. Mix those scents with stinky soap and you get the kind of stench that could make a skunk sick. This room seems to get smaller with each labored breath.

"Are you done yet, Doctor Hauschild?" Elizabeth says and adjusts her hands to get a better grip. "I don't know how much longer Herbie will cooperate."

"Your dog is not cooperating now, Mrs. Hartman." The doctor sprays my foot with the soap solution and wipes it clean with something that tickles.

I itch to tear out of the examination room door. My muscles jerk. Instinct tells me to fight. I'm caught. I can't flee. I snap my jaws shut before he has a chance to aim his spray bottle again. I crouch and bite down hard, and then release. The surface is supple. It's like biting through soft butter. I feel a modicum of relief. I am savoring the moment when I taste blood. You deserve this mister veterinarian, I growl and clamp my jaws tighter. I'm enjoying the moment until I open my eyes. I'm mortified to see pink flesh…Elizabeth's.

My jaw sags. My head slumps. I crinkle onto the once clean floor and howl. Horrors. The floorboards are cold on my fidgeting muscles: a bridge of relief in a flood of shame. I glimpse through wet eyelashes to see Elizabeth clasp her arm. I wince and draw my forepaws over my face, attempting to flatten into a membrane on the floor, a smaller target.

"I'll be all right," she says and covers the bite with her hand, but her eyes yield to tears. Stress fills her voice. "It's okay, doctor. He didn't mean to hurt me. Herbie loves me."

I belch yellow vile on the doctor's white floor. This must be what it feels like to have a panic attack. I want to gallop somewhere but my feet feel numb…must go…get away, but I can't move. Can't stand. I look up at a picture on the doctor's wall. In the painting a young boy is paddling a canoe on a river. The idea comes to me out of nowhere. "Wolf, can you hear me? Help me escape into my mind. Tell me a story? Wolf? Wolf, are you there?"

Walks Like a Bear, what do you want from this puzzle of trees and clouds on the doctor's wall?

"I need to hear your voice."

If you want to hear about the canoes, stop wiggling and curb the racket.

"Yes…about canoes." The scent from the disinfectant makes my nose scream for fresh air. I try edging closer to the opening under the door.

Walks Like a Bear, listen and remember. The bear clan was famous for building canoes. The Potawatomi built dugouts by charring the centers of tree trunks, then carving the insides with hatchets. Are you listening?

"My ears are open. Talk faster."

Birch bark canoes were formed by covering a framework of branches with bark, then sealing the cracks with hot pine pitch. The lightest canoes were covered with deerskin. The People of the forest used these narrow boats on lakes and on rivers to hunt, fish and to travel. Is that enough information?

"Thank you Wolf," I say. "I can make it on my own now."

Doctor Hauschild's knees creak as he unfolds from the floor. His scent is sweat tinged with anger. My eyes follow him as he stands, growing taller until his head stops somewhere near the ceiling.

The man bends in half to remove a black cowhide muzzle from a drawer in the bottom of his examination table. "If you can't control your biting, I will," he says to me, his seedpod eyes drilling into mine. "Is that what you want, Herbie?"

I growl an emphatic "No!"

"Be quiet." He locks the leather muzzle over my nose and loops it behind my ears. I am deeply resentful. First my foot and now he has compromised my jaw. The thought of hurting Elizabeth horrifies me, but resentment trumps my guilt.

Elizabeth's jaw muscles bulge. She pastes me to the table with the weight of her hips. She locks my head under her arm. I can't budge forward. "Herbie, you're not at home. Watch your manners" she says.

I don't know how to behave in a vet's office and I don't care to find out. I am blocked from moving backward by the doctor's brown boot. Conversation has ceased. Grunts and heavy breathing replace silence. Horror replaces resentment. Remorse follows, but disappears when blame emerges. I wiggle loose.

The powerful doctor should not have grabbed my back paw and tugged it towards him. I would not have bitten Elizabeth if he would have dropped my foot when he was warned. A dog doctor should understand canines do not like people touching their private parts.

Doctor Hauschild's eyes glow red and narrow into slits. "Herbie!" he bellows in his deep baritone. "Stop!" We struggle. He is on a tear. He wrestles with me until I am pinned, an unprecedented disgrace. At the bowels of defeat my free will disappears…a depth of despair no dog should have to experience. This unfeeling veterinarian should know to be gentle with a puppy. He should know words that soak into ears should be whispered, not yelled. I expect bad results. Powerless, my mind wanders. I wonder what Calle would say if she saw me now. I wonder if Potawatomi dogs let anyone touch their feet.

The doctor's chest heaves as he probes my paw. He tells Elizabeth she should be able to feel my feet any time without a struggle. "If Herbie were my dog," the doctor draws in a deep breath, "I'd muzzle him every night when you brush him." The doctor exhales. "He will hate it at first, but he needs to learn that you are the boss and he must obey." The doctor sucks in enough air during his next breath to fill a tire on Bob's car. "He should understand that he can't bite you when he wants you to stop brushing him, clipping his nails or cleaning his paws." Doctor Hauschild stops talking but continues with his heavy breathing. "He must learn to be patient." He forces a smile. The big man points to his own nodding head and makes circles with his fingers.

"I can read sign language and I am not manipulative." I growl and stamp my foot at the doctor's nauseating shallow brain. Does he think I'm deaf, blind and dumb? I lower my head and flatten my ears. My dam didn't raise foolish pups. My foot stamping grows louder. My eyes flick back and forth to follow their conversation.

"Herbie is a good dog, but he is also spoiled," says the vet.

"Spoiled?" Is this doctor nuts and stupid? I should have smelled that one coming, should have distracted Elizabeth. I stare up at the trunk of the man, provoked by where this conversation is going, annoyed with his arrogance. I have taken a bad hit, but I do what any Potawatomi dog would do in this situation. I find a channel, a new road and imagine myself busting outside and doing something raw and rough and risky like chewing a tree branch.

"It's as if he is saying to you," the doctor ignores my phantom chewing and continues to speak to Elizabeth, "I'm not going to let you touch my paw because it's not convenient right now."

I finish chewing my imaginary branch and work on an imaginary limb. In my mind I can taste the bitter bark. Saliva drips from my mouth.

Elizabeth is doing the growling now. "Doctor Hauschild, I don't think…"

"Let me finish, Mrs. Hartman." The doctor continues lecturing on the finer points of changing my behavior patterns while he probes my paws. I am now chewing the trunk of an imaginary tree. I flinch from the foot pain, and lose my concentration.

"Ah ha! This is what's hurting him," the doctor says, indicating with his head for Elizabeth to look at my left front foot.

I stop growling, listen with interest and attempt to turn my head to see.

"Feel this," the doctor says to Elizabeth and slams my head back flat against the cupboard with his elbow. "Dirt stuck to the hair between his paw pads has formed a hard ball. And here's a thorn…looks like it may have come from a rose bush. This lump would feel to Herbie like a stone would feel in one of our shoes." I feel him push my toes apart, squirt in some cold solution and gently massage the marble-sized ball until he pulls it out in pieces.

His elbow moves enough so I can twist my neck to see what he's doing. The doctor releases his weight, a relief because he's been crushing my chest to the cupboard. The pinching pressure and pain seem to be gone. I wiggle my toes to be certain. No pain. I step down to put pressure on my paw. No pain. This doctor seems to have fixed my foot.

The sensible doctor encourages Elizabeth to feel a second hairball in my right foot and shows her how to remove it. "You should try to keep this hair clipped short between his toes," he says while I watch.

So maybe this Doctor Hauschild isn't such a bad guy after all. He did make the pain go away. We've had our differences, but it turns out he's good for something. When the visit is over we step outside the good doctor's office. The storm has cleaned the air of the scents of disinfectant and soap. It smells like a new day outside…as fresh as raindrops. I skip along painlessly and watch rain water soak into pavement cracks.

At home Bob sits in his green leather chair turning pages of a magazine with a dog on the cover. I can smell his socks from where I lay listening to their chatter. Elizabeth reclines on the arm of his chair. She strokes his goat beard and stops to point to a picture using her bandaged arm. I can tell from Bob's glance he wants to pull my tongue out by the roots.

Each dawn during the next moon I lay near the end of the driveway to watch for the mail carrier. I am expecting a box with the worst: a cage for my muzzle. I refuse to cry, even inside my cheek. When the mail arrives, I push the brown carton into the bushes behind the mailbox and bury it in the neighbor's compost pile, the one with the rotting blue gills, the sleeping worms, and Bob's brown leather slipper.

Sometimes it's a good idea to relax, sit back, and think of all the people I would like to sink my teeth into.

TWELVE

The lake has become an empty prairie of open space, a forbidden adventure for me. A dog like me could race over this endless ice without ever turning a corner, could move so fast he could take to the sky like a crow, or be so far from home he could howl at the moon without being told to shut-the-hell-up.

How does water, so soft and tasty, turn brittle and slippery in a few short suns? The flavor of fish wanes, and smell becomes so hard and cold it bites my nostrils. Lured back out on the flats by sheer curiosity, I find the frosty crust slick and full of surprises. My rear legs fan out like the white tails did. I could never fight the wolf like that buck. I muscle my legs together, and stand. With each step forward I strain to hear a crack.

People waiting on the solid surface are sitting on upturned pails, holding short poles over open holes. I dash across the ice to take a closer look. Elizabeth's two-tone whistle echoes across the lake, a familiar signal for me to come at once. I see her arms move like reeds blowing in the breeze which is her sign for danger.

I respond at once skidding, sliding and dragging myself over the slick ice. I fall, smack my chin, scramble to my feet and collapse again. I find traction on patches of deep snow on the ice, but the going is sluggish. On a detour towards shore my legs fly in four directions at once. I don't see the opening in the ice until it's too late.

I hit the open water running. I must be living above luck level because I seem to be sprinting through the shallow water near shore. My chest pulses like a caught trout's heart. I scramble out and onto the beach real fast.

Elizabeth's sweater absorbs most of the cold water when I jump into her arms. Inside the cottage she dries my coat with a soft towel. During her hug I smell fear. She wipes the tears from her cheeks, a delayed reaction for what might have been. I can hear her heart pounding like it had during the strawberry moon… the last time the lake tried to drink me.

"Look Herbie." She points toward the window in the kitchen door. The Irish setter and German shepherd are watching outside the glass. "What do you suppose they want?" She opens the door and offers each dog one of my special biscuits.

"I thought he was half smart," Calle says to Beau and takes one of my Milk bones.

"He vill never make two seasons," Beau says to Calle. "Not on this lake." Before he sucks the other treat from Elizabeth's hand he shakes his head and says, "That chucklehead vould have been eaten if he had lived among the People." Together they withdraw from my kingdom, chewing my biscuits as they shuffle home.

"The Potawatomi eat dogs? That can't be true. Wolf? Wolf can you tell me if…"

THIRTEEN

I'm here, Walks Like a Bear, says Wolf.

"Tell me I didn't hear that right," I think to Wolf. "Tell me the truth. Did the Potawatomi eat dogs? Do they still eat them? Are dogs the meat filling in what Bob calls hot dogs…the ones he cooks on the grill? No wonder that brute likes them. Is that what happened to the dog before me? Wolf?"

Calm down, Wolf says.

"Wolf, I know Bob is my alpha, and he likes to eat, but he doesn't have the right of it. Not with dogs. Not with my friends…my family…"

Stop, says Wolf. *I'll tell you, but you may not like this legend. Listen and remember.*

"How could I forget?"

The People were kind to all animals, but they especially loved dogs. The Potawatomi brave, Maguesh, hunted, fished, and trapped by himself where the North wind lives. His only company was his pack of dogs, twenty in all. These hounds pulled a sled strong enough to move heavy loads of waubosog, beaver, mink, muskrat, and raccoon pelts across snow and ice. The Potawatomi hunter shared his morning breakfast with his dogs and provided each with a bear skin for a sleeping rug.

"Did Maguesh eat them?" I say and scratch my ear.

I recall another story about Little Pine, a great warrior who became a chief. Son of a Potawatomi woman and an English longknife quartered in Detroit, he lived with his tribe where he trained a pack of sporting dogs. They were his playmates. One dog caught small beaver alive and brought them to his hut. Others retrieved game he harvested in the forest or shot over the lake. The dogs traveled with him wherever he went and lived inside his wigwam.

"Wolf, did Little Pine eat his dogs?"

It was uncommon to eat pets except during ceremonies. It is true that dogs were sometimes sacrificed as an offering to the Great Spirit. Unless the tribe was starving, they didn't eat dogs.

"Sacrificed?" I crouch lower to the ground.

During the White Dog Feast a small, cream-colored dog nurtured for this purpose was sent to the next world. The dog had been decorated according to tradition by the Shaman, the medicine man of the village, to cure the illness of a member of the tribe. It was an unselfish honor to be chosen as the sacrificial dog because the dog gave his life to help another.

"Why were dogs chosen instead of cats?"

Dogs were considered extremely powerful. When a brave died and was on his road to paradise, a great dog guarded the path to make certain the warrior didn't return.

"I would feel a bit better about the whole sacrificial dog legend if instead of dogs they sacrificed humans, perhaps only people named Bob. But, thanks for the information," I say.

Elizabeth steps outside and calls my name. When she sees me crouched on the lawn she walks over and ruffles the hair along my back. "Relax Herbie. If anything happened to you, my heart would break." She kneels on the grass and holds my face between her hands. "I won't let anyone hurt you, but you must listen when I warn you to stay off the ice." She shakes her head. "I wish you could understand me. Come inside, honey."

I feel confident this female will prevent me from ever becoming a sacrificial dog, but I don't trust Bob. I notice a pair of tall boots in his closet. I wonder if this baby mouse I found is smart enough to climb out.

FOURTEEN

Snow covering the sunset road is a remnant of a winter storm that blanketed Clark Lake from one end to the other. Beneath the snow the road is frozen solid as deep as the roots of an old oak with iced ruts on top as hard as stone. Calle promised to take me down this road to see where the German shepherd lives, but that was three sleeps ago. I can't explain why she waited for the coldest day to show up in my yard, a day filled with purple storm clouds and plenty of bluster.

Travel down this road must be painful on Red Dog's calloused, leather-hard paw pads. I hobble alongside her picking my way between the ruts, the freezing weather deadening the pain on my tender feet. "Calle, are we there yet?"

We have been in the shepherd's yard only a short time before lightning flashes across the sky followed several heartbeats later by the rumble of thunder. The Irish setter sniffs the air, scans the sky and starts for home.

"Calle, I don't understand. Didn't we already walk this way?" I smell our scent in the snow, still fresh. "Are we leaving before we arrive, or, did we arrive already and are leaving before we see Beau Schmidt?" I sit in the snow, scratch my ear, and then get up and follow Red Dog. "I'm confused."

Our paws forge troughs in snow that is now falling heavily. It collects on our leg hair and hardens into icy balls. "Was that Beau Schmidts' house? I didn't smell him anywhere." Calle doesn't comment. Our shuffling feet grow heavier with each stride… like a snowball does when it tumbles down a hill. Moving becomes exhausting then slows to a stagger.

"I don't remember my wigwam being this far from Beau's Schmidts'," Calle says. Lightning flashes from a cloud as dark as crow's feathers. The spidery light is followed by a thunderclap that shakes the frozen underneath.

Nothing about our walking side by side distinguishes our breed or rank. Coated as we are in hair matted flat with wet snow, our eyes shut to slits against the wind, we might be part of any pack braving the weather for any number of reasons. We are barely distinguishable from each other, except that I do most of the talking.

"How long before we get home?"

"There are some, I am told, even among your admirers," Calle says, "who wish you would talk less."

"Calle?"

She turns her head. "I'm right here, Herbie. I'm the dog walking in front of you."

"I won't tell you what happened in my dream if you make fun of me."

"I'll be slavishly supportive if that's what you want." She pauses. "Don't drag behind."

I spill my guts about all that worries me. "I got emotional when the snow wouldn't stop and the limbs on the larch were struggling to hold the heavy mounds," I say trotting to catch her.

"Yes, go ahead. I'm listening."

"I heard a loud crack and a soft thud. A branch had given up under the weight, and let go. It fell to the ground exposing an open wound to the winter winds. When the tree whimpered I cried too. Is it unnatural for a dog to have such strong emotions for a tree?" I am uncomfortable exposing my weakness to Red Dog. I will howl if she laughs.

She responds without moving her head to look at me. "Herbie, the Potawatomi believe the tree is our brother. It is natural to feel sad when our brothers are wounded." She stops to look over at me. "Will you promise to report to me if you have any more of these unusual dreams?"

"I had another dream, Calle." Her interest encourages me. "Three sleeps ago the same blizzard was working itself up into something substantial." I edge close so the old dog can hear me. "Snowflakes were so large and close together I couldn't see the lake. One cloud looked like a plow horse crushing twenty puppies in one rush across the sky." Wolf had told me to watch for this vision and report it to Calle immediately. "Lightning flashed an image across the horizon that looked like a humpback raccoon bringing lightning bolts down on his enemies." I didn't follow Wolf's instructions and now I think the dream could be important. I sense danger ahead. "Calle, are you going to die?"

She stops. "Yes, it's true I am having trouble with death, but I won't leave you today. The signs you described say it will be soon. Did you see anything else?"

"Yes. I saw a sudden white flash, a bang and a lightning bolt that hit near me in my dream. It shook the ground." Remembering makes me fidget and my ears itch. "Then the blizzard restarted and we had another whiteout, like this one. Are you having dreams, too?"

"Sure. I have vague, pointless scraps of dreams that lead to this place or that, but nothing like yours." The setter looks up at the sky and picks up her pace.

My chest feels tight; I'm growing alarmed we may have strayed off the road. I continue talking to hold back my panic. "After that dream," I say, "whenever it snows I stay inside the cottage and consider my character flaws. Calle, you told me courage was being able to meet danger without giving way to fear. I'm afraid nearly all of the time. Does that make me a…a coward?" There, I have exposed another bleeding truth.

Calle stops moving in the heavy snow and turns to me. "The Potawatomi call a coward a Waubosog, the word for rabbit. It is an insult to be called a Waubosog." She glances behind us. "Herbie, do you hear something?"

"Please concentrate on what I'm telling you. Being a coward feels so natural to me. I must have been born gutless. You see, I'm worried I won't have the nerve to do my job if a dog tries to fight me or attack Elizabeth? What if a wolf attacks? Will I flee if I face danger? Will I hide? Roll over and pretend I'm dead?"

"Most of the stuff dogs worry about never happens," Calle says. "Besides, you're still young. You have time to develop courage."

I smell danger. It could be close, it could be around the next corner, or my nose could be mistaken. If I warn Calle and I'm wrong she may not want to believe me the next time. What should I do? I'll take her advice. I won't worry about it. I'm glad the storm has started blowing again and Calle can't see my face or hear my teeth chatter.

"Excuse me Herbie. Is that the sound of a station wagon?"

I cock my earflap. "I don't hear anything. Calle, are you listening to me? Courage depravation could be serious for a dog my age. I've seen five moons."

The old dog continues walking.

"Calle, did you hear me?"

She turns her head but continues to walk. "Herbie, sometimes silence is the best answer."

I continue talking. "During the last blizzard I was cold and wet. I grew nervous watching the wind blow snow into mounds. The temperature rose and the snow turned to slush, then rain, and then into an ice storm. A thick crust blanketed the deep snow. As I rushed outside to pee…"

"Excuse me, Herbie, but I hear a motor and it's coming this way."

"Calle, please listen. This is important. I crashed through the hard top of the snow. It was so slippery down there I couldn't keep my feet together, couldn't even stand long enough to lift the leg I use to mark rocks and I had to go. I was helpless under the snow crust skidding around. I knew no one could see me or help me; I had to find my way out or freeze. I used my paws to dig a tunnel towards our cottage, at least I think it was in that direction."

"Excuse me for interrupting the longest confession of terror and trepidation I have ever encountered, Herbie, but I think the motor sound I hear may be the snow plow."

I pause to listen. "No, it's not the snow plow," I say, dismissing her observation, "but it might be the mail truck." I continue walking and talking. "So then a branch from the trunk of our pin oak crashed down through the snow crust from directly above me. It had been frosted heavy with a load of snow. I jumped to avoid it and scraped my belly on some ice."

"Excuse me, Herbie, but I'm pretty sure it's the snow plow."

I stop to listen. "No, it's not the snow plow, but it may be the garbage truck. Calle, after that branch incident that almost killed me I shook inside for the rest of the day. I had felt sad for my brothers, the trees, but they turned on me. That pin oak nearly pounded me into the landscape."

"That is contemptible behavior for any tree," comments Calle, breathing hard. She is puffing along with great effort. Her paws, heavy with snow, beat out a rhythm: pick up, pace, put down. Snow seals her eyelids. Pick up, pace, put down. Steam shoots from our nostrils in regular intervals.

"Let's stop and rest a while," I say. I watch our breaths rise in the icy air like clouds as we wait in the snow. "Sheep dogs are bred to be tough," I say, "to live with sheep in all kinds of weather."

"I've heard that rumor," she says, takes a deep breath and coughs.

"Our breed is supposed to look and act like sheep. If a wolf attacks the flock, a sheepdog is supposed to protect the herd by killing the wolf. My sire told me that."

"Excuse me, Herbie, but if that is the snow plow, we should move off this road or it will plow us up into a snow bank."

"I'm not sure we're on the road, Calle."

"Where are we?"

"Lost."

"We must be on the road. Otherwise, why would the snow plow be coming toward us? Hear that?" she says. "I'm certain it's the snow plow. Can't you hear scraping over the hum of a motor?"

I am so focused on sharing my fears with my friend that I continue to ignore her observations. "We sheep dogs are taught to be strong but never to be ruthless. I'm more like a frightened lamb than a fierce sheep dog, except I smell better."

"Your fragrance today is elegant, like decaying seaweed," Calle flatters me. She is still resting on what she thinks is the road.

I try to see around and between the snowflakes to determine what's making that grinding racket. "Calle, you're right. It is the snow plow."

I grab my snow crusted friend by the nap of her neck and attempt to lift her, but with all those snowballs stuck to her leg hair she is no match for my muscles. Calle is as heavy as a boulder. With a sudden surge of adrenalin I jerk her up and over my left shoulder just as the silver blade slices the snow at our feet.

FIFTEEN

I don't remember much after that until I lick my nose. It's cold, which is a good sign, healthy for a dog. But my belly and feet are cold, too. Then I recall the snow plow.

"Calle? Calle, where are you?" I listen but there is no answer. The snow isn't packed hard. "Calle, are you dead? Please answer me." I can move my back legs, but the rest of me is held by a weight heavier than mine. Could I be buried alive? I whine for help, listen for a response and whine again. Nothing. I hate it when no one is around to help me. I find a piece of hard ice when I jiggle a back toe, wedge my paw and push. Grunts, snorts, and a long, sucking sound later I wiggle free of the mound of snow, shake and look around. It's snowing harder than before. I can barely see across the plowed road.

"Calle, are you in there? Have I killed you?" I charge around the heaping mound until a soft grunt pulls my attention to a lump near the base. "Is that you?" I plow my nose into the crust to pull out her scent, searching with hope in my bones. "It's you. I can smell rotten fish. You're alive." Honing in on her musty smell, I pull my snout out to catch a breath and see a red flag feathering from near the top of the snow bank. "Is that your tail? I'll dig you out Calle. Walks-Like-a-Bear is on the job. I will save you."

I try digging but the snow is packed hard at the top of the white mound. "Calle, I'm going to pull you out by your tail." The red tail wags harder and faster, but no sound comes from below. "Hold on my friend. I hope that's your tail." I grab hold of the waving flag and pull. Red hair comes out in great gobs. I stop to listen but hear nothing. If this is Calle, she clearly isn't feeling chatty. I dig all around the tail, my paws moving chunks of packed snow like a hungry tongue lapping kibble. Snow flies between my legs and out over the plowed road. I grab what's left of the flag between my teeth and give it another jerk. A chunk comes off. I have part of her tail in my mouth. I pause to spit red hair and tail bone from my mouth long enough to hear a muffled "Ouch!" from deep in the snow bank. Then I hear a shallow whine. The snow around the tail stump turns red.

Digging deeper I find her rump. I grab what is left of the base of her tail and with great effort drag her bottom out into the daylight. I stop to rest, but don't see her torso or a head. It's then I hear her say, "Easy does it, big guy. It's the cold season. Leave some fur for me. Don't chew out my bung hole."

I dig around her hind quarters until all but her shoulders and head are visible. I plow my muzzle under her belly, lift the old dog to safety and flop down to catch my breath.

"Nice recovery," Calle says after she shakes herself free of snow, "but I seem to be bleeding. Is that my tail over there?"

I stifle a laugh. "I must have pulled too hard." It's a nervous laugh. "I'll pack some snow around your tail stump. This has been a ripping wild day."

"I'll just sit on some snow. Thanks."

I get up and continue moving snow with my front paws until the cavity where she has been wedged is a cavern large enough for both of us to squeeze back inside. "It's another white out," I say. "Better wait in here for the storm to end."

Calle takes a look around, barks her agreement, and drags her tired carcass back inside the snow bank. She circles three times and settles her bones on the packed snow. The old girl tucks her nose under her back leg and falls silent.

"You okay?"

"Hum." She lifts her head, her eyelids twitching. "Thanks for the lift."

"Can we talk about courage?" I say, and curl up beside the red dog.

"Get some rest Herbie."

"But Calle…I can learn to be brave, I know I can."

"Herbie, can't you see that it took courage to save me from that snow plow?"

"I got you into this mess. I knew we were lost but was afraid to tell you…and then I pulled off, I didn't mean to pull part of your tail off…so it doesn't count as courage. I want to learn to be brave without hurting anyone, the kind of bold heroics that happen without fear."

"Spare me the drama. Let's not try this again. I only have one tail. Go to sleep, Herbie."

I scratch my ear. "I should practice growling."

Calle lifts her snout and shakes a yawn from her open jaws.

"GRRRRROOOOOOLLLLL! What do you think?" I say.

"Herbie, I need some quiet time."

"But Calle…I'm almost grown and I'm scared most of the time and…"

Red Dog lifts her head and looks me straight in the slits where my eyes should be. "Is courage your favorite obsession?" She yawns. "Go to sleep, Herbie." She stuffs her nose under her back leg, and pushes her rump into the back wall of the cave where the snow is still white. She is snoring before I catch her message.

SIXTEEN

"Calle, wake up. Move your paw off my nose!"

"Bojo Herbie. Is it still snowing?" The red setter stretches her back legs straight and pushes her paws into my belly. "You're nice and warm. Mind if I keep my feet here?"

"Yes I do mind." I'm feeling grumpy. "Stay on your side of the cave." I haven't slept much. I've been keeping the tunnel open in case her tail hole continues to bleed and I have to drag her out to safety…wherever that is. I don't tell her, but I'm afraid I won't remember which way to dig when the blow is over. Besides, Calle O'Riley has the eeriest snore. It's like a vacuum cleaner sucking small stones off a carpet. The entire night had been like a bad dream at an animal kill shelter.

Calle kneads my belly again and then quickly removes her paws. Her playfulness stops as she stares with empty eyes into the side wall of the snow cave, like she's remembering. And then she grins like a cat.

"WHAT IS SO FUNNY?" I wiggle to expand my space. I am hungry and cross. I need to stretch my cramped legs, but there is no room in the cave and the storm is still raging outside. And I'm thirsty.

"I am recalling an old Potawatomi legend," she chuckles, patting the wall on her side of our snow cave.

"I don't think being stuck in a snow bank is funny, but if the legend is about how a dog keeps warm in a blows-sideways storm, I want to hear."

"You've almost guessed it. This story is not just about seeking refuge inside a snow cave. I'm laughing because I never thought the legend would apply to me, I mean you and me, here, today." Calle grins. "You're in luck, my friend: I'm rested, and I remember."

"I'm tired and as dry as dust. Is the storm in the story as bad as the one howling outside?"

"Worse. This legend is about natives and their dogs marooned in a storm just like we are." Calle rearranges her feet on my stomach until she is comfortable and begins telling the tale.

"A long time ago native people learned how to survive being stranded in the open during a blizzard. They learned from watching their dogs. Selecting a safe location was the main concern. It was best to choose a sheltered spot where you wouldn't get buried by drifts. Native dogs simply curled into a ball, tucked their noses between their back legs like you are doing, Herbie. They fanned their tails over their heads, if they still had tails, to keep their teeth from chattering while they waited out a storm. A dog's winter coat was heavy enough to keep him comfortable except when the weather dipped to the extremes. In those cases dogs would dig a cave like you did for us."

"Did native dogs keep a tunnel open for fresh air like I am doing?"

"No. They could breathe through the snow as long as the snow wasn't packed tightly. When people of the First Nation were caught out in the open during a blizzard, they followed the example of their dogs and curled inside their black bear robes. Heat from their bodies kept them from freezing solid like ice."

"Did all natives wear the fur of the bear, Calle?" Without waiting for an answer I fire another question. "How many hunts did it take to produce enough fur skins to keep an entire clan warm for the cold season?"

Calle smiles. "Good questions. The grandfathers tell of night hunts on the river during the moon when the ice melts and trees sprout buds. They said a hundred black bear gave up their lives for the Potawatomi while being stalked from canoes lit by torches."

"Can bear swim?" I remember being told bear were powerful. I scratch my ear. "How did they catch them in the water?"

"Great hunters and their dogs used their minds to survive… like you must, Herbie. One legend tells of scouts who saw tracks of a great many bear during the moon of falling leaves. They were crossing the Grand River in the direction of the sunset. The men knew bear needed to store fat to feed their bodies during winter hibernation so they tracked them across the Grand River to their hunting grounds. Scouts reported seeing black bear forage for food on the prairies where the buffalo herds graze. Then they saw bear return in great numbers at the same river crossing in the moon of the first snow.

When the time was right scouts were sent to watch and report the beginning of the return migration. Hunters paddled their birch bark canoes upstream from the crossing. They waited in the rushes.

"The bear floated high in the water because of their winter fat. They crossed the river together like a school of bloated fish. Potawatomi scouts edged their vessels into the flotilla of bear and shot arrows deep into their necks. Carcasses bobbed in the bloodied river until the hunters could tie them to their canoes and tow them to shore.

"Women and children assembled on the riverbank, skinned the bear carcasses and carved up the meat. Litters made from small trees were strapped to the village dogs and horses, to the children and the women. Hunters piled pelts into their canoes and paddled upstream to the village while other men strapped skins to their backs and trekked home overland. Everyone helped lug the bounty back to the village."

I interrupt Calle. "Since they were the largest animals the braves hunted, would…"

"No, they were not the largest, nor were they the most dangerous."

"I thought you named me Walks Like a Bear because I am the largest and most dangerous dog in our neighborhood."

"You must not be listening because I told you this before. I called you Walks Like a Bear because you walk like a bear. If you were the largest and most dangerous animal, I would have given you the name, Shuffles like a Buffalo."

"Buffalo? Calle, do buffalo live in our neighborhood?" She doesn't answer. She must be asleep.

SEVENTEEN

I stretch my neck up the tunnel opening to the heavy snow. With a sweeping glance I look for… for the…and then stop. I squeeze my neck back down the fresh air vent and ask Calle what buffalo look like. "Are they larger than squirrels? Do they attack in packs like the wolf? Do they eat dogs?" No answer. "Calle? Wake up. Buffalo could be dangerous. I need to know."

Red Dog is sick and old and must sleep.

"Wolf, is that you?"

No, it's someone else.

"Wolf! I'm serious."

Okay, I will tell the legend.

"Thank you. I believe Calle remembers. She just needs a nap and she may have lost a lot of blood. You should lighten up on…"

Walks Like a Bear, if I want an opinion, I'll provide one. Now listen and learn and remember this forever. Buffalo have not lived on Potawatomi hunting lands for many seasons, but they did at one time. A great Eskimo wolf dog, a husky called Shunka, shared the Peoples' fire circle and hunted buffalo with them. She was whelped many seasons before Barks at Birds was born.

"Who is Barks at Birds?" I scratch my ear.

Regretfully, she was a rather silly dog and holds but one distinction: she was the first dog to pass along the legends many winters ago.

"The other one, Shunka the Eskimo wolf dog, how did she die?"

Walks Like a Bear should be asking how she lived.

My head drops. I am embarrassed by the smallness of my thoughts. "Wolf, tell me about the life of the husky, Shunka."

Listen and remember this legend forever. Shunka lived with the game scout, Wapasaw. Are you listening?

"Yes, yes Wolf." I scratch my ears with my back paws.

Shunka was so tall that when she walked by Wapasaw's side she came up to his thigh. She had a long, narrow face, erect ears and a long tail that curled over her back. A thick undercoat kept her comfortable when temperatures dropped well below the instant when water becomes hard and slippery.

"I know that season," I think.

The Bear clan was starving that winter. The cold had been brutal and their stored food was gone. Wapasaw went into the forest on his snowshoes to hunt game. He wore a fox fur hat and wrapped himself in a long buffalo robe. Below his heavy buckskin leggings he wore two pair of moccasin. The inside pair were stuffed with buffalo hair to keep his feet warm. The second pair were larger and worn with buffalo hair on the outside to keep his feet from freezing to the wood and reed platforms that kept him from sinking into deep snow.

One morning Wapasaw's trusted dog, Shunka, caught the scent of buffalo. Wapasaw was half a day's walk below the village on a scouting trip, not far from here, when Shunka ran to him and pulled him to a ridge that guarded the lake.

"I know that ridge," I say. "It's across our lake on top of a sharp incline."

You're right, Walks Like a Bear. Instinctively, both Shunka and Wapasaw lay flat on the ground. From their position at the crest of the ridge they could see a large herd and could feel the breeze on their faces. The herd was upwind so the buffalo couldn't smell them, become agitated and stampede. The enormous animals were crowded onto a splinter of land jutting from the south shore of Clark Lake on what was called Eagle Point.

"I know that splinter of land across the lake from us. I've heard it called Eagle Point. Elizabeth and Bob bring back delicious hamburgers from a restaurant there. I know more than you think I know. Wolf, what is an eagle?"

Eagle is chief of all the winged creatures. He flies higher than any other bird and sends a message to those who see him to have courage, explore, and continue to learn. Walks Like a Bear, if you listen and remember the legends Calle and I tell you, your vision will be wide like the eagle. If you remember the legends forever, you will be able to tell others so they can reach beyond what they thought possible.

So, in this legend the shaggy brown animals chewed the bark from tall cottonwood trees where many of the mighty bald eagles nested. They chewed willow swale, blackberry bushes, and whatever scrub brush they could find. The snow was deep. Food was scarce for them, too.

Wapasaw crawled backwards from his viewing post without making a sound. He had counted the herd and was anxious to report Shunka's find. Soon they were at his village. The scout howled the game-scout wolf call, a sound so terrifying it could stop the hearts of anyone within hearing range. This signal told other game-scouts that he was about to enter the village, and that he had been successful in his scouting mission.

The next morning Wapasaw awoke first. He loaded his quiver with sharp arrows. He would need strength for the hunt so he ate a piece of the pounded and dried meat called pemmican.

"What does pemmican taste like?" I scratch my ear.

Walks Like a Bear!

"Alright, I'll just listen and remember forever. But I am getting hungry and my ears itch."

Shunka blinked awake in her sleeping nest outside Wapasaw's wigwam. She stretched herself and sniffed the air. The smell of the herd was strong. She ran into the wigwam and jumped on Wapasaw.

The brave told Shunka she smelled like a herd of buffalo. He gave the dog a piece of the dried meat, but the dog wouldn't eat. Shunka pulled Wapasaw outside by his leggings where the odor from the herd almost knocked him over. The scout understood just how near the herd was to his village. Shunka told her she was the best hunting dog in the clan and stroked her long, narrow head. He gave her his last piece of dried buffalo jerky. He called to the hunters that the attack must come downwind from the herd.

"I would have liked Shunka," I say. "She must have enjoyed chewing that dried meat. I know I would enjoy chewing a piece of dried buffalo jerky. It must be delicious."

Walks Like a Bear, listen or I will tell this legend to that snowflake.

'Yes, Wolf.'

Wapasaw led the hunting party in single file into the forest before dawn lit the sky. Each brave followed with his dog. The scout's steady pace led them south of the village, around the sunset end of the lake, then to the ridge where they could view Eagle Point. A large herd grazed in the deep snow on the peninsula of land.

'Woo, woo, woo' was the signal from the throat of the game-scout to the hunters positioned around the herd. On cue, dogs barked and howled and charged the buffalo. Braves followed wailing so loudly and war-whooping so fiercely they scared one another.

Startled, the buffalo grew confused. Some stampeded toward the east, others west. All were uncertain which way to escape. The snow-covered lake was the escape route the herd chose. They plunged onto the prairie of ice. The herd's momentum carried them far from shore where they were again confused and ran this way and that. The hunters within range shrieked war cries and emptied their quivers. The herd swept toward the opposite shore. Many dead were left behind pierced by the hunter's arrows. They lay in black mounds on the frozen prairie. Some from the herd escaped onto the lake's north shore.

It was a successful hunt for the Potawatomi. Once more the village would eat well until spring. A happy chant came from far out on the lake where Wapasaw unsheathed his knife. He began the work of skinning and cutting the meat into pieces small enough to carry on Shunka's back and on his own shoulders.

"How much of that delicious buffalo meat could a dog Shunka's size carry?"

Walks Like a Bear! Do you want to hear the legend or ask questions?

"I just wondered. I'm a little peckish…didn't eat breakfast."

All the hunters were busy working when one brave called attention to a change in the weather. 'The morning sky has turned deep blue, the sign of a blizzard.' He pointed towards where the north wind lived. 'We must hurry into the nearby woods before it reaches us.' Some heard his warning, passed on the signal, and then hurried towards the woods where others had already arranged crude shelters and gathered dry wood for fuel. Around the campfire the half-starved hunters sat and stood, while slices of savory meat roasted.

The storm enveloped them in its whirling whiteness. 'Woo, woo!' they called to those who had not yet reached camp. One after another answered, and in the end the only ones missing were Wapasaw and his husky, Shunka.

"What happened to Shunka?" I think.

I'm getting to that part, says Wolf. *Be patient and listen.* One of Wapasaw's friends said, 'I know he will be all right. He is brave and experienced. He will find a safe place in the storm and will join us when the wind dies.' They wrapped themselves in their robes and lay down to sleep.

All that night and the following day the storm raged. Late the second night the storm blew out. The hunting party awoke to a thundering quiet. It was so still they could hear the thumping feet of hungry jack rabbits echoing down the slopes. The air soon filled with wolf howls and coyote yelps. Packs of the ravenous creatures rushed onto the ice and ripped at the snow covered carcasses.

Braves scrambled and slid onto the ice. They shouted war whoops and waved their weapons at the foragers feeding off their kill. Wolves worked in packs to drag the meat across the ice and onto the north shore.

Hunters moved further out on the frozen lake to recover their bounty when they heard the hoarse bark of Shunka, the missing scout's dog. They moved towards the sound and heard the muffled war-whoop of a man, as if it came from under the ice.

"Wolf, please hurry and tell me what happened to Shunka. I'm so hungry."

Walks Like a Bear, I will not tell you again. Listen! The braves approached their friend's voice. The sound came from near two buffalo carcasses the wolves had dragged to the sunrise end of the lake. Shunka was seen hovering over one of the mounds. The dog staggered and fell when the braves arrived.

Hearing Wapasaw's voice, the men attempted to pull open the hide covering one buffalo's belly, but it had frozen shut. Using the sharp blades on their hunting knives, they found the lost man in a warm nest of buffalo hair wrapped in his own robe. The scout had placed his dog in one of the carcasses and himself in another for protection from the storm. Shunka was wiser than her master. She kept her entrance open. Wapasaw had let the hide of his carcass freeze shut, confining him inside.

Hunger drove the wolves to the dead buffalo at the end of the lake. Shunka climbed from her frozen hideout to protect her master from the wolves. She was surrounded and outnumbered. Part of the pack dragged Wapasaw's frozen shelter over the slippery ice while the loyal Eskimo dog followed and fought for her caged master. When the hunters arrived they found the wolves had been driven from Wapasaw's buffalo carcass, but it was too late for Shunka. Her wounds were fatal.

Freed by the braves, the scout stepped from the buffalo skin with a face anxious for his loyal friend. 'Where is Shunka, the bravest of our clan?'

'Here,' said a fellow scout pointing to the ice stained with Shunka's blood.

Wapasaw knelt beside his dog, stroking her narrow face. His heart was hollow. 'My friend,' he said, 'go to where the Great Spirit lives. I will meet you there.'

He carried her body to the woodlot overlooking the lake. The scout scattered red sand over her burial mound as was the custom, and the Bear clan's farewell song was sung. Since that day this place in the woodlot has been known as a sacred burial ground for dogs with soongetcha, strong hearts. Walks Like a Bear? Why are you so quiet now that the legend has an end?

"Where is this burial ground?"

You will know when the time is right.

Pulling my back legs gently from under Calle, I push my snout up the tunnel to inhale fresh air and find a sky filled with stars. The wind has grown tired and gone to sleep. I climb out. Calle is a heartbeat behind me.

"Let's go home," she says.

"Which way is home?"

"I thought you knew. Herbie, we're not …"

EIGHTEEN

"Lost. Just say it, Calle. We're lost again. I'm such a terrible…"

"Oh stuff it, Herbie. Why didn't you explore while I was sleeping? What were you doing all that time?"

"Wolf told me the legend of Shunka and Wapasaw."

"Good," she says. "Remember it so you can tell all the animals. It is part of our history." I hear her stomach growl. "It's time to eat. I wonder if my family missed me. I wonder if they will ever find me."

Calle old girl, you were wondering?

"Wolf, I'm so happy you still listen for my questions," Calle says.

"I'm wondering too," I say to Wolf. "Calle and I are here in this snow cave because on the way back from Beau's yard I lost the road because of the storm and then Calle heard the snow plow but I didn't think…and then Calle was lost in the snow bank and I thought she was a goner and then I pulled her tail off…"

I know, Herbie, says Wolf. *I watched it all happen. You should know by now I'm always watching over you, and Calle too. You're both lost and Calle's bleeding has stopped for now.*

"Right. What do you mean for now?"

Her tail hole is frozen. She needs to go to the doctor when it defrosts. Your families have been looking for you since you've been away, Wolf says. *The storm has slowed. Follow the fresh path Mrs. O'Riley left in the snow. You're not far from home. Herbie, you must help the old girl. Her back legs are weak from the cold. Go now before it begins to blow again. You will know the way.*

Calle follows the double line of tracks that mark the snow near our cave. I have my muzzle between her back legs, holding her rump in the air and pushing her forward.

Calle stumbles and lands on her face. "Not so fast, Herbie," she growls as her head snow plows along the tracks.

"Sorry," I say. "Can't see much under here." I stop until the old girl regains her upright position. It doesn't take long before she recognizes landmarks.

"I think that's our hedge…under that snow bank. That may be our white house behind it."

I push with my muzzle until Calle cries, "That's the O'Rileys' entrance door." When I remove my nose to look Calle is scratching her signal on the wood door. I hear screams of delight all around when they see she's safe.

"Where were you, old girl?" Mrs. O'Riley shouts. "Calle, I missed you." says the oldest boy. "Me too," says the middle son. "I missed her more," says the baby. "No, I missed her more," says the daughter. Mrs. O'Riley rubs the sensitive fur behind Calle's ears. She strokes her head and checks her paws for frostbite. I can smell dog treats in her pocket. "We've been looking for you and Herbie on the snowmobile. Come on in girl. Come in. Can't you walk? I'll carry you…what happened…where's your beautiful tail?" My belly chimes like a clock. "You better go home now, Herbie. Your family is worried about you, too. Calle, I'll carry you inside. We've got to get you to a doctor."

Calle is happily wiggling her bottom. Her tail hole pain is frozen for now. She doesn't notice when the door shuts leaving me standing outside in the cold. It's all right with me that she forgot to say bojo. She probably forgot to save me a dog treat, too. I wonder if Bob will celebrate my return. I walk around the fence, across my yard and bark my signal.

"Herbie!" Elizabeth screams and charges into the cold to greet me. "Are you okay? Are your feet frozen?" She kneels in the snow and feels my paws and nose. "Where have you been? You know you're not allowed out of the yard." She orders me inside the kitchen.

Didn't she see the sun dial I left in her garden? I made one just like Beau Schmidt showed me before…the blizzard. Ah…the snow tricked me and covered it. Or, was it Wolf?

"Where is your friend Calle?" Elizabeth bends down to kiss my nose. "I knew you would be smart enough to find shelter inside someone's house next to a nice warm fire." She dries my feet with a big white towel and rubs my belly. "You're lucky you didn't get trapped out there during the blizzard. It was nasty." She picks up the phone and calls Mrs. O'Riley. "Herbie came home. Is Calle safe? What? How could that have happened? Yes, please let us know. Goodbye."

Elizabeth would have accused me of inventing stories if I had told her we had found shelter inside a dead buffalo's hide. Nor would she have believed the snow plow buried us and we had waited out the storm in a snow cave. She would have thought me loopy if she knew an invisible wolf had helped us find our way home. So I bark that Calle and I were twirled by a twister wind that dropped us in a tree top. We slid down the trunk with a bump, and shortly after that the blizzard stopped.

Elizabeth laughs. "Herbie, sometimes I think you understand every word I say." She gives me a lamb and liver dog treat and a bowl of warm beef stew she made for Bob.

I am so comfortable with my belly full that I fall asleep and dream about pulling Calle's tail off. Instead of blood coloring the snow, it shoots up like it was coming from a garden hose. I wake up with a start and can't fall back asleep. I lay there in the corner of the bedroom thinking about that silly old dog called Barks at Birds who lived so long ago. Wolf said she had leaped into the Milky Way from the same sacred burial ground as Shunka, the first dog with the strong heart. I wonder if dogs can leap into the sky without tails when they die.

NINETEEN

The sky is especially dark over Calle's cottage today. A black cloud lurks there shadowing her wigwam, an ambush. Thunder rolls and rumbles. Lightning flashes. Gloom ladles down covering our cottage too. Blue shadows lurch into black holes behind the wicker chairs. I'm home alone.

According to Beau Schmidt, a thunderstorm is unusual when it's bitter cold like this. He said the Potawatomi call thunder, *baimwawa*, like the fiery explosions sound. I imagine the ear-pounding crashes to be a dog with large feet stumbling overhead, rushing and then retreating, being pursued by an even heavier dog with feet the size of pumpkins. I race from the lake room to escape the thumping, slamming, and hammering. I attempt to hide under Bob and Elizabeth's bed but get stuck. It takes most of the morning and some of the hair on my rump to work my way out.

Being a coward takes too much time, too much space in my head, and too much of the hair along my spine. I try to remember which legend will help me move forward, build my confidence and bring honor to my breed. When Elizabeth comes home, she finds me wedged between her bed and the wall. She lets me outside for my afternoon toilet. I won't hide there again.

I would have practiced marking trees, but my back leg was sore from so much of Beau's vertical homework and cramped from being stuck under the bed. I still have not mastered Beau's perpendicular pee. Since no dog is watching, I walk behind a rose bush and squat in the rain. But the Sycamore, within clear view from that angle, has a screech owl posted on a branch. I shake myself empty and hustle to find Calle. I must report my sightings as promised.

Mrs. O'Riley is in the boathouse moving kayaks, canoes, and family toys for warm weather moons. The overhead door rumbles closed as she dashes through blowing snow towards her cottage. "Calle, I'm cooking rice for you," she calls over her shoulder. "It will make your tummy feel better." Scents of cooking meat slip out the kitchen door before she pulls it closed behind her.

The old retriever had told me once that Potawatomi women and children used canoes like Mrs. O'Riley's to gather wild rice. And like Mrs. O'Riley, they boiled it in water for their families to eat. I wonder where this grain grows and if Mrs. O'Riley gathers it to feed her family.

Walks Like a Bear?

"Wolf, is that you?"

Of course it's me. Who else would talk inside your head? I heard you wondering, again? I will tell you the legend of rice if....

"I know the rules. I won't ask too many questions, and I will listen and remember forever."

Right. One interruption and it's over. Agreed?

I nod and scratch my ear.

Natives harvested wild rice that grew in shallow lakes not far from Clark Lake. Stalks carrying the wild grain grew high, taller than a person in a canoe can stand. Long before the rice was ripe, the Potawatomi edged their canoes into the forest of stalks to bend and tie the long stems together. Bundling allowed the winged creatures to eat the outside seeds while saving the inside grain for the People. During the harvest moon natives returned to the shallow lakes. They beat what grain was left from the bundled stalks into their canoes, and transported the black seeds back to their village. Rice that had been dried in the sun was stored in deerskin pouches and buried in pits for their winter store. Bojo, Walks Like a Bear. I must go.

"*Bojo, Wolf.*" I am wondering where I can dig a hole to find one of those deerskin pouches of rice when it occurs to me that Calle is nowhere in sight.

"Calle?" I hear her grunt, check her wigwam, and hear her moan. I enter without permission and smell sickness. "Calle, last time we were together you were a dog. Now all I see is a bag of bones." She doesn't smile. I step closer. My friend's nose is pale and scaled so dry it has cracked open. "Did you drink some bad water?" Peeling skin exposes her raw, pink flesh. She is curled into a ball, shivering. I take my place on the straw with my eyes lowered and break the hospitality rule. "Calle," I say before being addressed by her first. "May I touch your snout?"

"No," she whimpers. She is as hoarse as a frog. "My nose feels like it has been slammed in a door and my rump pains me. Herbie?" I lean close to hear. "Is there an owl roosting in the Sycamore?"

I don't tell her about the owl. Smelling big trouble, I look at her feet and notice ice packed between her swollen toes. I back from her wigwam and dash for Mrs. O'Riley's door.

"Calle's got frostbite!" I bark so loud the crows fly from their nests. "Open up. Calle's got frostbite." I scratch the wooden threshold.

Mrs. O'Riley looks irritated as she swings the front door open. "Herbie, what's this racket about?"

I grab her sleeve and drag her to Calle's wigwam. "Here," I bark, pushing my black nose into Calle's paw.

"Ouch! Herbie, you did that on purpose!" Calle croaks. "Ouch! Ouch! Ouch!"

"Calle, honey, what is hurting you?" Mrs. O'Riley says as she kneels down and looks inside. "Oh sweetheart, your nose looks bad. Oh my, your paws are puffy. You lost your tail bandage. Calle dear, you need to go to the veterinarian again. You have more than an upset tummy. Come inside, my poor pet."

The old dog hops on three legs to the door. "Ouch! Ouch!"

I watch Mrs. O'Riley help her inside with her arm under her belly. I remember Calle's question and glance up. A bird perched on the lowest limb of the Sycamore is staring down at all that's happening with yellow eyes. It has a white throat swatch that continues into a thin V down its chest. I recognize the bird from Calle's description…a horned owl. On the ground beneath the branch is an accumulation of undigested bones, fur and feathers, a sign this sycamore has been its roost for some time. I turn to tell Calle, but the kitchen door has closed. This is my second sighting.

Many suns come and go before I see my old friend again. She is sunning on the O'Rileys' sidewalk when she explains how ice-melting dust the yellow trucks spread on roads made her sick. "I was cleaning my feet like I always do," she says. "The same doctor who cut the frostbite from my paws and stopped the bleeding on my tail stub is making me well. I didn't expect my belly to hurt like this. It feels like I've been kicked by a cow. After our walk each day I get my feet and stomach washed. And, I get to sleep inside with my family," she says which explains why I can never find her outside on especially cold nights. I follow my friend as she crosses the yard to her wigwam.

"Calle, you have lived many winters and are so smart," I say walking into the darkened wigwam. "Why did you let the frost bite your feet?" She is curled into a ball on the straw. A beam of sunlight from her door searches for lice on her stiff, gray coat.

"Well, Herbie, sometimes you get, and sometimes you get got. Some dogs die from tooth infections."

"How do you feel today?"

"Somewhat unremarkable, but, any day this side of the flower bed is a good day for me." She scratches her ear with a back paw and then stands and walks out into the sunshine.

Calle has been well since the moon of the snow crust, a season when the sun warms the top of the snow into a firm skin before it turns it to mush. The lake ice has been thick and heavy this season, holding flat the cheerful summer waves.

Calle glances up. "What's that?" She hunkers down. Fear flows from her eyes.

"Oh, that. It's just a horny owl."

Red Dog crouches, her knees tremble. "Owls can see in the dark," she whispers.

"Lots of animals prowl at night," I say. It frightens me to see my mentor show fear. "I smelled a skunk after the sun dipped below the tree line." It's my fault. "I saw an opossum around the same time." I promised her I would alert her right after I saw the owl in the tree. "I saw a raccoon prowling at night, too." I could have saved this old dog stress. I am a terrible friend.

Calle is usually so in-charge and confident. "The large fowl roosting in the tree looks like a stuffed owl to me." I grin at my cleverness. Red Dog is not impressed. "Elizabeth's cooking dinner. She's looking for a winner to cook for dinner." She doesn't respond to that one either. I'll try the truth. "Calle, the owl has been here while this moon has lit the night sky. Why are you shivering? Are you cold?"

"Think, Walks Like a Bear," Calle says. "Owls can see things others do not. Owls are wise. They are the link between us and the Great Spirit."

I can see bad dreams coming.

"In the tradition of the Potawatomi, owls serve as messengers," she says. "When they enter your space, they can see the coming of death. They come to warn it will be soon, usually before the next moon."

"That's a dreadful legend." My eye begins to twitch.

"One of us has been summoned," she says.

Since she is so old, I am inclined to think it will be her. It couldn't be me, could it? "Calle, let's kill that old owl."

Red Dog settles into the snow and gives the sign for me to curl next to her. "The owl is the messenger; a service the Great Spirit assigns it. He is only doing his job. Don't hurt the night bird."

"But, I hate that owl," I say, annoyed that all of a sudden it's hard to breathe. I hope this isn't another panic attack. I lay down. "I hate the way its beak is hooked and the way its eyes are staring." I may vomit.

"Hate is like a snake swallowing its own tail, my young friend. It will consume you in the end. Calm yourself. Now look at me. Take deep breaths in sets of three, three times." She breathes along with me to demonstrate. Calle waits until the third set when I finally get a grip, arranges herself on the fresh straw Mrs. O'Riley has arranged in her wigwam and curls nose-to-tail. Before she falls asleep she mumbles, "Herbie, remember this: If you find yourself in a hole the first thing to do is stop digging. Can you remember that?"

I scratch my ears then lay quietly in respect for the one whose bones are brittle and teeth have grown long and yellow with age. I leave my old teacher snoring and creep home.

TWENTY

The sky becomes clear and bright and bitter cold. It's meaner on my feet than a bee sting. My toes prick hot like I've stepped in a fire of pine needles.

I return to Calle's wigwam. We exchange pleasantries as I prance in place to displace the pain in my toes. Her feet, frostbitten some time ago, must still throb. She nods me to my place on the ground and distracts my obvious discomfort with chitchat.

We discuss deer tracks in the snow outside her wigwam as she licks my paws to soothe the pain. We talk about vines the deer have chewed to the root while she massages my feet with her muzzle. We speak of a mound of deer scat and plan to roll in it later to disguise our scents. Small talk.

"Calle, How do you know so much about this band of Potawatomi?" I've been pondering this question since the day I met her. "They are human. You are a dog." She jerks a delighted look at me and nods me inside her wigwam. When we are curled together for warmth, she covers my paws with loose straw and tells me the legend.

"Many winters ago, a stray pup wandered into a Potawatomi village not far from here." Calle's breath forms fog as she speaks. "The pup was welcomed, fed, and became part of a pack of dogs living with the People native to the land which surrounds this lake."

Straw falls from my feet as I shift to get comfortable. "Where is their village?"

"Nothing is left but burial mounds and a few arrow heads." Calle recovers my feet, patting the straw back in place. "They lived in a hollow between two hills along a trail at the crest of a ridge. Log cabins and wigwams that looked like large turtle shells were built around three small ponds. The wigwams no longer exist." Calle rubs her paws together to stimulate her own circulation. She yawns. "I'll just shut my eyes for a short …nap, and ….ZZZZZZZ."

"Were their wigwams like this one?" I say. "Like yours, Calle? Calle! You can't nap now. Not now. I want to listen and remember forever. Calle!"

Walks Like a Bear.

"Is that you, Wolf?"

I've been talking to you for months. Your ears are among the largest in this neighborhood, yet you can't recognize my voice by now? I've got to talk to Calle. I had a feeling this wouldn't work. I should have told you from the start.

"Told me what?"

About the mistake. Calle said she would help and you never would need to know.

"What mistake?"

It's all my fault, says Wolf. *Entirely.*

"Wolf? If it's about me I should…"

Yes. Yes, I agree. You should know. Okay. That day I saw you swimming in the underwater. Do you remember? You were just a pup. I mistook you for a muskrat. Beneath the lake's surface you looked like a wet rat. The muskrat's den is below your seawall… by your dock.

"Why were you looking for the muskrat?"

Calle told me this muskrat was trainable…had the potential to learn and remember forever. He was clever. I tried to find him to bring him with me but his den door was washed closed by the waves. That's when I accidentally found you. Personally, I think Calle was premature in her retirement plans. Her memory isn't as bad as she thinks it is.

I tap the sleeping dog with my paw.

"What? What's the matter?" she says, suddenly awake and sitting up. "Herbie, I was having such a beautiful dream, and…"

"Wolf is here," I tell her.

"Where?" Calle sits up. "Wolf?"

Can you hear me, old girl? Wolf says.

"What's this about? Why did you wake me? What did you tell Herbie?"

He knows.

"Calle," I say. "Wolf thinks I'm a mistake. I'm no mistake. I can be clever if I try harder. I have potential. I can listen and remember forever. Give me another chance to develop my courage and use my channels to make change. I want to be strong like a bear. I want to listen and learn…especially on such an overcast day when my feet are stinging and there's nothing else to do. Come on, Calle. Please give me another chance. Just look at my ears. They're raw from scratching them every time I remember."

Calle says nothing. She lays her chin on her feet like she is about to fall asleep again.

Walks Like a Bear, Wolf says. *Calle says you are doing just fine. She says I should tell you the legend of Barks at Birds. She says I should stop meddling.*

"Good idea," I say to Wolf. "Calle was telling me about wigwams when she fell asleep. It happens in the middle of a story and it's so irritating when I don't hear the ending."

Walks Like a Bear, listen and remember, and do try to be quiet. It's so irritating when you interrupt the story. You could help me by asking your questions at the story's conclusion. Questioning is good, but it's a matter of me becoming distracted and possibly forgetting to tell you an important point.

I scratch my ear. "*I'm still learning to listen and remember, but I'll…*"

Okay. I get it. Spare me the chatter. Wigwams were built like large turtle shells…much larger than Calle's doghouse. Village women worked together using young saplings stripped of their branches for the walls. Working in teams they buried the large ends in a circle and fastened the flexible tops.

Calle crosses one forefoot over the other, shifts her shoulders and listens.

The framework was covered with birch bark to make it waterproof. Inside, the floor was layered with mats woven by the women. Animal skins served as sleeping blankets.

"I could never sleep on a dead animal's coat, or on a dead person's hide," I say to Calle.

"You have a thicker coat than most animals," Calle says. She pushes my long shawl aside inspecting it closely. "I wouldn't mind sleeping atop a hide like yours."

"Don't get any ideas. I'm lumpier than I look."

Do either of you want to hear the rest of the story? Wolf says.

The retriever smiles and winks at me. "I'm not done sleeping. I'm going back to catch my dream."

"Wolf? I'm ready. Wolf? Wolf, are you napping too?"

No, I'm attempting to learn patience, and you are a wonderful teacher. I was telling you about skins. Native women cured animal hides by rubbing the fat off on flat sandstones. They dried the skins in the sun on rocks and stretched them to cover their homes. Small holes in wigwam walls brought sunlight inside so women could do fine beadwork and basket weaving. The round smoke hole in the top doubled to catch light and as a vent for the cooking fire.

Calle snorts, and scratches her ear with her back foot. "Expect the worst and you'll never be disappointed." She yawns, speaking to no one in particular. "Be careful, Herbie, Wolf has a claustrophobic world view of the bear clan pack of canines." She rolls to her side.

"She's dreaming," I tell the wolf. "Sometimes she talks strange when she's tired. Sometimes she walks her legs while she's sleeping, or wiggles her nose. She used to twitch her tail before the…"

Calle used to be quick-witted, a stand-up sort of dog, but now she's close to barking mad, Wolf says.

"Just tell me the legend," I say to Wolf. "Don't insult my friend."

Okay. The People knew how they fit in their world, like you are learning, Walks Like a Bear. They respected the land and the animals. They shared their community stewpot with strangers. But the old ways were dangerous and required them to spend most of their time looking for food. The old ways changed when the pale-faced settlers arrived and claimed Potawatomi hunting lands as their own. Natives sold their animal pelts to traders for exotic cooking pots, warm blankets, thunder sticks and a drink that gave visions.

"Wolf, do you remember that stray pup that wandered into the Potawatomi village long ago, the first to tell the legends. Was her coat cream-colored like mine?"

No, Walks Like a Bear. She was not the sacrificial animal, but a special dog I will tell you about. Sacrificial dogs were especially chosen for this path. Understand this. A dog born with a cream-colored coat is not marked for sacrifice. Just because an Old English sheepdog is born with a gray and white coat, it doesn't mean it must spend its life in the show ring or a field herding sheep. Each pup given life has a different path. Each pup must find the forest trail that fits its heart.

Your other question was about Barks at Birds, Wolf says. She came from mixed parentage, what we call the American breed. Her look lay somewhere between a cream-colored beagle and a yard dog, like a fox in the face but with fuzzy red hair and a black mustache. When she was old enough the pup was taken with the Potawatomi hunters as a hunting dog in training.

She would follow the braves noiselessly into woods, Wolf continues. She would wait without moving for hours. But when the pup sighted pheasants, a partridge or a guinea hen, she grew so excited that she lost control and barked, and barked, alarming the wild birds. Fowl flitted into the forest before the hunters had time to haul out their arrows. Geese and ducks sought refuge flying towards the sun so the hunters would be blinded when they aimed their weapons. Birds warned the squirrels who whispered to the waubosogs who told the deer that Potawatomi hunters were looking for volunteers for their evening stew pot. The scouts were angry with the pup and refused to take her with them again. They scorned her and gave her the name Barks at Birds.

"Wolf," I say. "Can any other dogs in our neighborhood hear you?"

Only Red Dog and you, he says. Calle tells the legends to everyone, but few will remember. Walks Like a Bear, you must remember them all.

"Can dogs or humans hear what I'm thinking?" I scratch my ear.

I am the only one who can always read your thoughts. Dogs and people can hear when you want them to, when you speak to them in your head, when you hold your body a certain way or by the sound of your bark or howl. Sensitive, intuitive, and intelligent people can understand what you want most of the time. But most humans understand up to the level of a dog in its third season.

"I'm hungry, Wolf. Can we talk about food?"

Right. While the sun slept the Potawatomi scouts speared fish by the light from torches mounted on their canoes. When the sun smiled they twisted line and hooks made from shells. They harvested the fish from the lakes and rivers. They dried their catch in the sun and stored the dried fish for winter. They snared and shot small game, sometimes using steel traps and thunder sticks purchased from the Indian traders. They harvested deer by stampeding them into corrals where they were caught in spring-loaded tree traps hidden in the underbrush.

I'm drooling.

Women and children planted fields of maize, beans, and pumpkins after burning the forest and tilling the soil. Sap was drained from maple trees and boiled in clay pots during the moon of falling leaves. Maple sugar was saved to sweeten food during the cold winter moons.

"Does maple sap taste salty?" I ask Wolf.

Walks Like a Bear, have you tasted trees?

"Just the bark at the bottom. It's salty."

Maple sap leaking down the tree would taste pure and sweet, not salty. You didn't taste the message trees, did you?

"Do you mean the same trees I lift my leg on? Those are the ones that taste salty. Why?"

Smell messages. Never savor them. What you tasted was… oh, just don't go around licking any more history trees. Do you understand?

"I do get it." I scratch my ear with my back paw. "I wonder if my old salt-licking alpha will complain when the beans and pumpkins from Elizabeth's garden taste salty?"

TWENTY-ONE

Elizabeth says etiquette is essential if we are to be good neighbors. She talks endlessly about dog manners on our walks. She says there will be no digging in our neighbor's lawns or flower beds, no marking of car tires or boots left outside on porches, and especially no jumping on babies in strollers. She points out examples of being impolite. A dog should not chase a neighbor's cat off the end of a dock, should not jump on old people wheeling walkers and especially should not nip jogger's heels during a triathlon.

Elizabeth says we must be civil at home as well and can never say 'thank you' enough. For example, she rewards me with a, 'Well done, Herbie,' after I do my business on our lawn. I do understand. As an example I wiggle between her and the wall when she sits on the toilet. I let her scratch my back while I wait for the flush. And then I back out and give her a congratulatory lick on her knee. That's being polite.

I can handle Elizabeth's neighborhood etiquette, but it's entirely another matter to try to match the manners of Beau Schmidt, the canine she holds up as an example of excellent behavior.

The dog's alpha, a man called Doctor Schmidt, takes great pride in Beau's training and good manners. The black and brown German shepherd comes when he's called even if it's during an important fetch-the-stick game. He moves to the side of the road and sits when a car passes. He heels on command. Elizabeth is in awe when she sees Beau's display of willing obedience. The peculiar scent of her admiration smells like the putrid powder Bob sprays inside his old shoes.

Beau Schmidt has polish. Something about the way he swaggers when he walks attracts my eye and draws my attention to his muscular round haunches. Something about the way he holds his chin… tipped slightly up, makes him look like he has substance. Something about the way he cocks his head to one side when I'm barking shows he's listening and makes me feel important. When Beau pauses before barking or eating, he gives eating and barking more significance. The dog has great style, but sadly, he makes me look bad.

Beau is a large dog with bones like massive tree limbs ribbed evenly from his shoulders to his hips. The shepherd is always clean, well-brushed, with ears free of mites and unsightly hair. I have never seen him scratch a flea. He looks strong, well filled-in with muscles in all the right places, yet is as gentle, good-natured and good-humored as a baby kitten. A natural leader, he is the chief watchdog that watches over all the other watchdogs in our neighborhood.

Today as we near his house I hear the rumble of his snoring before we discover him lying on his back in a deed sleep. All four of Beau's legs reach for a sun blazing directly overhead. Sap from a pine tree has been dripping from an overhead branch, landing on the dead grass near his head. Not one drip has disturbed him.

A black squirrel studies the scene from the Scotch pine above. A waubosog waits for the drama to explode under a hydrangea bush. Elizabeth and I sense some excitement and stop to watch from the side of the road.

Ordinarily when the German shepherd senses an intruder in his yard his instinct to protect takes over. He jumps from flat on his back to airborne attack in one flowing movement. It has happened to me before. It took less than two blinks. Before Beau's feet hit the ground and I was trucking down the north wind road as fast as I could haul. His growl convinced me gnashing teeth would be followed by brutal disfigurement.

Calle told me his instinct works the same when he's shaken from his sleep. Before he is totally awake his response to an intruder can be frightening, especially from such a large dog. But Beau is always gentle with neighbors and family… when he eventually wakes.

Today, it turns out, will be no ordinary day in the German shepherd's yard. The sun is heating the pine pitch above Beau's head. The sap sags. I can see the nosy black squirrel edge out on the pine bough and look down at the sleeping dog. He steps into the sap and like a fly stuck in a spider's web, attempts to lift one sticky foot at a time in vain. As the squirrel struggles to free his feet and keep his sense of balance, he moves closer to the end of the branch. The branch bends. Large lumps of melting pine pitch roll down the limb taking the squirrel with it. The rodent's sense of balance slides down the branch with him until he's hanging by one sticky paw. A small slug of sap leaves the main gob in a string, growing longer with the sun's warmth. The black squirrel whirls his tail around the branch to save himself. His paw is stuck in the sap, and now his tail is too.

Beau's raw instinct for protecting his space kicks in when the first string of sap hits his nose. His head snaps up. He swivels his muzzle and sniffs for the scent of an intruder. His growl says it all: he will rip away the flesh and chew off the bone stubs of whomever is out there, yet he remains horizontal.

As the sun moves between the clumps of leaves overhead, its heat softens the sap into syrup. The string stretches to the ground, and the lump at the end of the limb lets loose. The squirrel's black tail stretches, slips and the squirrel falls.

About then is when my ear begins to itch. Before I can scratch it I glance up to see the squirrel drop, and look back to see Elizabeth gawking, taking in the scene with eyes the size of black walnuts. I hear the descending squeal of the compromised squirrel. He's heading straight for Beau Schmidt.

Beau rolls to his feet when he hears the squirrel's squeal. His ears fold flat to his head. He crouches ready to spring when the bulk of the sap hits his head. His muzzle lowers with the weight of the pine pitch, his teeth clench in surprise.

I can tell he is not fully awake because his eyes remain closed. I can tell he is flying on instinct alone when the squirrel's four sticky feet land firmly on his rump and he calmly glances back and gives the squirrel the stink eye. I'm not certain he's sleeping when his roar of defiance shakes the ground.

The black rodent falls from Beau's backside and hikes it up the tree in record time. The waubosog vanishes down its hole. Elizabeth and I fall over one another backing down the road to flee from the ferocious dog.

I know Beau won't hurt us once he's awake so I jump in front of Elizabeth to protect her. I look directly at him while we back away. He advances.

"Beau, wake up." I whisper so I won't make him angry…in case this entire drama is a joke. "Beau, it's me, Herbie." I take another step back.

He shakes his head like a dog does when a tick crawls under an ear flap. The tremor on his head quakes its way down his back. The hair on his spine stands straight up at attention all the way to his tail…not the sign that says I'm a particularly friendly dog. Beau Schmidt cocks his head to one side and looks at me clearly for the first time.

"Walks Like a Bear?" He nods an acknowledgement at Elizabeth and addresses her with a, "Good day, Mrs. Hartman," bark. Beau's ingratiating smile turns into a controlled hiss of irritation when he looks back at me. His white paws are standing in sticky sap that has slid from his skull. His sneer is followed by a ferocious growl.

"Nice teeth," I say, and take a quick step back. Beau gives me no ground. He snarls. I take another quick step in retreat. My amusement starts innocently enough when he ceases the threatening growl and wiggles the bulb on his big, black nose.

I consider the involuntary movement at first to have been caused by a bee or a bug drawn there for the tree honey. The dog's thin black lips draw back; his pink tongue lengthens and overlaps his nose licking it clean. A broad smile spreads across his muzzle before the sneeze comes. The sudden jerk of his head propels additional sap down his muzzle and into his eyes. He blinks then attempts to paw it clean. He smiles again. This is a sign he's joking, having fun at my expense.

Beau's smile flits away like the bug that was never there. He starts for where he thinks I'm standing, snarling, his teeth flashing, a rumble gurgling from his throat. He misses me, stops and holds his nose high while he sniffs the air.

I stand my ground until unruly spurts of glee escape my muzzle, and explode into great, honking guffaws. My knees shake. I sink to the pavement and roll onto my side.

Beau checks his attack, but continues his long, low yowl. He glares down at me while I roll on my backside, kick a dance in the air and howl.

"Herbie?" says Elizabeth. "What are you doing?"

Trotting my feet high in the air, I pause, and roll to my belly. I'm shaking in merriment. I bang my paw on the pavement over and over to release the belly-laughter cramping my stomach. I gasp for breath. I have finally found a chink in Beau's perfect German armor.

This great dog can make a mistake. Like the rest of us he will attempt to save face with an offensive move and then go on the defense when that doesn't work.

Beau is scratching the sod with his back feet. Plugs sail through the air. Beau's teeth flash in the sun. His crouch gets lower. The dog is ready to charge. Meanwhile, his tongue is licking the sap. He rubs his muzzle on his chest. He licks his nose. He tongues under his chin. His tone lowers to a stern growl.

My howls cycle higher and lighter.

"Herbie, stop it. What's wrong with you?" Elizabeth fidgets, keeping her distance from the vicious shepherd. "Come away from that sick animal. He may have distemper." She's begging now. She pats her knee. "Come, Herbie. You're acting strange. You're scaring me. I better have the veterinarian look at you." She takes large leaps backwards while keeping her eyes focused on the action.

I am gleefully doubled over until she utters the veterinarian word. I am instantly sobered and about to beat a fast retreat when a miracle occurs.

"Beau!" A stern shout comes from the Schmidts' side porch.

The shepherd freezes. His ears jerk toward the sound. He snaps his sticky head around.

"Come!" says Doctor Schmidt.

Beau spins on his back legs, fires across the road and careens inside the cottage leaving his rage hanging behind him in mid-air, vigorous and menacing.

Not one of us makes a move or breaks the silence until a wabasog emerges from its hole. The rabbit glances around the yard, wiggles his nose and retreats just as fast as he appeared. The black squirrel stays at the top of the Scotch pine licking sap from his tail. I turn to see Elizabeth dashing down the road without me.

My reaction to Beau is severe amusement. I have never observed irritation defused so rapidly by an angry dog as when he greeted Elizabeth. I have never seen a retreat so timely and swift as I observed when he heard Doctor Schmidt's command.

I catch up with Elizabeth at the bend in the road. I can smell the scent of putrid foot spray before she says a word. I hate that smell of admiration. "Did you notice how quickly Beau obeyed?" she says "He's such a well trained dog. Why can't you respond like that?"

"Fish feet!"

TWENTY-TWO

Stiff from a snooze on patio stone, I stretch, hump my back and push my front legs flat. I stretch again and slump my spine like a sagging towel on Elizabeth's bathing suit drying line.

I hear a squeal from inside the lake house. I sense no great passion or urgency in Elizabeth's scream, so I stretch on my toenails doing the lazy cat reach.

I hear a screech! I can tell its Elizabeth screaming. My next stretch is the squirrel tail curve.

"Herbie," she shouts. "Help me!" she shrieks.

This seems an odd request from my guardian during a scream. I take a drink from the open water by the artesian well.

"Go away!" she yelps. "Will somebody please help me?" Elizabeth's wail sounds needy. I can hear her bawling. "Where are you Herbie?" she cries.

It hits me like a blast of wind. Elizabeth's life is in danger. This woman needs me, me… the cutest puppy in her world, me… her little honey dumpling. So that's how it works.

During one heartbeat, I am a puppy and Elizabeth is my mentor. She teaches me to move to the side of the road when a car approaches, to step back from danger, or drop everything and come to eat. She coaches me to heel by her left knee while we walk. She shows me where I should relieve myself in our yard so Bob won't step in it, and to avoid knocking over the UPS driver and the gas meter maid when they enter our territory.

A heartbeat later she thinks I am capable of avoiding unsavory people walking our roadways and protecting her from who knows what? How about that? This shift in my universe makes me feel grown, gives me purpose and perks my ears. I'm excited.

Herbie the Love Bug has become a responsible sheepdog. I can feel my chest expand. I promise that black squirrel watching me from the hickory nut tree no matter the cost I will protect this woman. One heartbeat has made all the difference.

I can't move toward her until my butt stops wiggling. My head jerks from side to side and jackknives out of control like a semi-trailer on one of those highway overpasses that look like tangled tapeworms. I fish-tail until a gusty wind wags me tight, and coils me into a spring like the one that holds the screen door closed. I unwind from the butt-coil spinning, reeling around as a pine tree blur follows a pine needle blur that morphs into a dizzying yowl blur.

"Herbie!"

Harnessing my enthusiasm, I breathe deeply, and wonder if an intruder is hurting Elizabeth, or if a wolf is threatening to pull her into the underlake. Perhaps the house is on fire and she needs me to pull her from under a fallen timber. I sense the pleasure of responsibility, of having a vital function in my family. I am in good-dog ecstasy; my head's swimming in self-importance. I can at last do the job I was bred to do: protect my pack. I race to the doorway where my mistress is waiting.

"Herbie, there's a mouse in our house," she says. "It's in the bedroom closet. Do something!"

"Flounder feathers," I growl. "Is that all?" My chest deflates with a gush of air. "I wonder how that fuzz ball escaped the old goat's boot."

TWENTY-THREE

Doctor Schmidt is organized, well-mannered, and precise, just like his dog. He commands the kind of house where all the towels in the bathroom are arranged in a row. A tall lean man, I'd call him weedy… all elbows, ears, and whiskers, he believes everything the family owns should have a purpose and a cupboard location. When the Schmidts' closets bulged past capacity, Doctor Schmidt hired a bulldozer to dig a hole in the red clay behind their cottage for a new storage building. While leveling mounds of greasy clay for the foundation, the dozer tracked the fragrant mud over the pavement between the building site and cottage. The slick smudge dried into fine red powder.

My feet are stained red from our daily walks. Elizabeth's shoes are smeared scarlet. But Beau's four white boots remain clean and well groomed, just like Doctor Schmidt's salt-white hair. Several times each sun the good doctor washes Beau's paws in a bucket kept for that purpose on the side porch.

"Herbie, why can't you stay clean like this dog?" Elizabeth says, pointing to Beau. Here comes that smell again.

It is later under another sun when I'm walking Elizabeth. We are trotting down the sunset road by Beau's house. Doctor Schmidt is supervising a truck dumping the gritty material that he tells Elizabeth is for the building's foundation.

"Hey! You okay?" I say to Beau. He is his old self again, feeling frisky. He romps with me in the sand.

"Finer than frog hair," says my good friend. We dig holes in the gold grit, chase each other in circles, and flop around like dying chickens.

Two men push the sand evenly into the hole lined with red clay, moving forth and back, spreading it until it's flat. Workers pour what looks like the thick gravy in canned dog food into the depression and trowel it smooth. Straight lines are cut across the silvery surface giving it an organized, all-in-a-row look like Doctor Schmidt's bathroom towels. Elizabeth bends down to admire the neat edge on the newly poured floor before she calls me to go home.

Beau and I are wrestling on the cottage lawn, boxing and barking. Elizabeth calls my name again. Beau teases me with a stick. He barks and chases me in circles. The big dog pokes me, gooses me, and entices me to take the wooden stub, but I'm tired of the game and besides, Elizabeth has called.

I trot toward the edge of the shiny gray surface to investigate what she has been examining. The workers have gone. Beau prances along behind me, ready to pounce and reinvigorate our competition. I pick up speed as I draw close to the flat groundwork. Beau is close behind.

Elizabeth recognizes the impending disaster. "Herbie, come this way!" she says, and looks surprised when I skid to a stop and obediently run to her side.

Beau Schmidt just keeps on coming. His lateral form is sheer perfection as he launches into the soft concrete. The smile on his face dissolves as suction holds his front feet firmly in the mud. His back legs puncture the muck, entering past his front elbows. His chest and face enter last leaving an upturned mass of German shepherd with a tail curving round on top. Pulling his nose from the muck, he leaves a deep impression of his muzzle. When he shakes away his concrete mask his look of shock gives me more satisfaction than one of Elizabeth's homemade liver treats.

Beau whimpers, then misfires some gas he has been holding back. The atmosphere is now as befouled as the dog. The murky mess has spattered his legs. The goop has gushed between the toes on his four white boots. His once pink belly is the color of puppy poop. Beau coughs, then glances behind him. He howls deep despair as he stares at the trail of paw prints behind him, across his guardian's perfectly poured floor. I see the dog cringe. He must have realized his error, and Beau Schmidt never makes mistakes.

My friend is holding one soiled boot in the air and whining when Doctor Schmidt's voice booms from inside the door of his bungalow. "Beau! Come! Let's eat!"

The mud spattered dog wades in the gray sludge toward his guardian, extracting one foot at a time from the ooze. I hear a loud sucking sound before Beau plops his foot back into the slop. Suck up. Plop down. Suck up. Plop down. The scene could have generated a good laugh had it not been for the broken look on Beau's face. Suck up. Plop down. He stops to send me a look, "I thought you were my friend," then plods on. Solid ground at the edge provides a base to shake and distribute bits of wet concrete across the remainder of the poured floor and produce a line of tracks across the lawn to the Schmidts' clean cottage.

Elizabeth and I hear shouting as we scramble toward home. I hear Doctor Schmidt scream at Beau. We increase our pace to a gallop.

My guardian explains why a dog must not walk across fresh concrete until it has hardened as we run home. Beau's paw tracks will be like fossils on the floor forever. Then there is the matter of the Schmidt's kitchen carpet.

Dusk filters up azure from the lake. Dark blue shadows pool in the undergrowth by the seawall. Owls hoot in the near distance. Beau's howls trump the dusky hue and bruise my heart. This German shepherd is my friend. I could have warned my teacher to stop before he plunged into the wet concrete. I have never heard him cry before.

The Hartmans are sitting by the lake enjoying the night air when I slip in between them. Beau's misery becomes mine. Elizabeth senses my mood, massages my shoulders, and rubs my back. "Herbie was an extremely good dog today."

I try to smile.

The old pleasure-seeker frowns. "Wouldn't it be considered an oxymoron to mention Herbie and good dog in the same breath?" he says.

"Bob, give the dog some credit. Today I had this feeling someone was watching me…a funny sensation I sometimes get in the back of my neck. I know it's nothing. I looked around but didn't see anyone. I just felt safer having Herbie by my side."

Words like these mean more to me than rolling in a perfectly putrefied fish.

TWENTY-FOUR

It is the moon for suckers, a time when small fish struggle against the current to spawn up ice cold streams. Wind pulls warmth from animals sleeping outside when the sun is hiding. But when the morning sun teases the midday sky the effort to stay alive becomes bearable. That blazing dot appears and distributes hope equally among us. It makes the snow sparkle. Dreary days turn inspiring. Heated rays settle on each section of my spine as it slowly clicks into place, each spinal tick separating my dreams from the real.

Calle's barking disrupts my rhapsodizing. "I'm going to the vet," she says. "I'll see you when the sun replaces the moon."

Elizabeth's barking interrupts Calle's disruption. "Herbie, come! We're walking at the Ella today."

"Calle, wait!" I bark, concerned about her illness, but when Elizabeth's words hit home, my eyelids began to twitch. Stop! Everybody hold it. I only just opened my eyes. This is too much information before my morning stretch. Give me a moment to organize my thoughts.

"Come on, Herbie. We'll be at the park," Elizabeth tells me, "so you can play with your friend, the Dalmatian."

My heartbeat races. The thought of that dog makes me feel like a kitten in a dark alley encountering an angry pack of street dogs. I don't know which way to run. I crawl under the hydrangea bush and crouch. My toenails dig into the ground. I squeeze my eyes shut to disappear. My sunlit ecstasy frizzles flat. My enthusiasm drains into the ground like spring water swirling down the driveway drain.

"I don't want to go," I whine. "I cannot go," I howl. "Don't make me go," I groan. "Forget responsibility. Forget any promises I may, or may not have made. I don't want to see that dog with spots and dots again. I would rather struggle up an icy stream to watch fish spawn than go to the park today."

Walks Like a Bear!

"Is that you Wolf?"

Face the enemy. The first part of dying is giving in to fear.

Ella Sharp Park's meadows and woodlots are so extensive a dog can race at top speed without hitting flowers or fences. When the moons are warm the park has soft, smooth grass on the soccer and softball fields. But when the moons are cold the park is the most beautiful. Trees are white. Shrubbery is covered in white. Paths for walking dogs are spotless. Hardly any people use the park in the winter, so if we arrive early, it seems like my guardian and I are the first to step into this part of the world. At one time in my life it was my favorite place to hike with Elizabeth.

When I hear the park's name uttered now, dark dreams overtake my sleep. Blue-black ghosts drop from the sky and target my black and white spots. Phantoms reach down with lethal black claws, sinking curved talons into the tender flesh along my spine. The dreams are always the same: I'm flown high and then dropped. I hear the sharp snap of my neck and the crunch of my bones when I bottom out. I can see the vultures circle overhead. I can feel them picking meat from my carcass. I can hear them stop to gossip like they must do at their Sunday family brunches.

* * *

The dreams began three suns ago after a walked with Elizabeth at the Ella. We had crossed the snow-sprinkled soccer field and were resting near a red cedar where a horny owl perched. A sassy young Dalmatian dashed from the white pine woods, wagging her tail in welcome. She flashed me a look that would stir any dog.

The black and white dog returned my pleasantries with lowered eyes. Her mouth opened just enough to let her tongue list to one side before she pushed her tail straight up. Announcing her passion for fun this way was the only introduction I needed. Our legs, matched in length, allowed us to compete in a flat-out race. We jumped on one another, tumbled in the grass, barked and snorted. Turns out she was crazy about coconut macaroons too.

"How did you get so many black spots on your white fur?" I asked, comparing hers to my own patchwork hair.

"How did your black and white hair get so long?" Spot said. She zigzagged circles around me.

Elizabeth introduced herself to Spot's guardian and we continued our stroll together. The Dalmatian and I played as we hiked. The women followed behind exchanging dog stories and training tips. That was when the clouds opened and the sky dumped disaster on us.

I remember the sky darkening, a flurry of cross-directed winds, and the pulsing vibrations of all those flapping wings. I recall the feel of warm urine on the ground beneath me as the birds screeched and attacked us. Spot barked and drew her ears flat against her head. Her hair stood tall along her spine. Her tail stood straight out of her haunches, her body was lowered and her spotted nose was wrinkled back revealing white teeth. She was ready for battle.

She jumped and snarled at the winged demons as they circled, their talons like weapons trailing under their bodies. The birds maneuvered to get their claws close to the spots on the young female. She twisted. She turned. She ducked each time talons were lowered. She snarled with her teeth bared. Her lips drew back in a nightmarish grin. She almost toppled a huge, vicious crow, jumping and catching the bird's wing in flight.

In my worst night-sweat I have never imagined a winged beast as large and menacing as the demon that targeted me. I whined in terror. I scrambled around like a poisoned mouse unable to find a drop of water. My tail would have tucked if I had one. I ran. The crow gained on me. It came so close I could see the little wrinkles around its eyes.

Elizabeth appeared behind me. My next worst night terror was watching her strike the crow with what she was carrying–a plastic bag full of my excrement. I cannot imagine a more menacing combatant. The sight and sounds this poo-flinging female made as she danced across the grass, shouting, and swinging her arms was alarming, especially for me. The projectile-throwing Elizabeth stomped spastically, she shook her fists at them and flogged the flying creatures with my feces. I didn't know she had it in her. She was always so gentle at home.

Spot's guardian came running too, but wasn't nearly as frightening to the crows, or to me as Elizabeth. The air was full of screeching birds when somehow a truce was called and the ravens lit in the tops of the pine trees where the horny owl was still perched. Spot and I collapsed close together crawling over the grass and under Elizabeth's shadow. We sat quietly until our hearts slowed and our breathing became normal. I called the dread-filled event like it was…a moldy pigeon liver kind of experience I never wanted repeated.

* * *

So here we are after this balmy sweet sunrise looking at a new day already filled with trouble. I'm facing my worst fears and Calle has gone off and left me. Elizabeth is acting strange and unseasonably happy. I'm doomed.

"The Ella is where you can walk without a leash, remember, honey bunny? You can exercise your legs forever before turning around and running back to me." She pampers my head with her hand. "There are no burrs to catch in your coat or briars to snag your leg hair." She scratches behind each of my ears. "And, if you tire of large spaces, we can walk on wooded paths." She takes my head with both hands and locks my eyes. "Don't worry, Herbie. It's cold. The crows have all flown away." Her smile broadens as she drops my head. "Want to go?"

"No."

"Get in the car, Herbie. Now!"

At the park Spot is nowhere in sight, but I am, and I'm illuminated on the lawn by a bright sun. I feel small and vulnerable under this vault of blue sky. My black and white spotted coat quivers, a perfect target for the meanest birds of the species.

The crows have no trouble finding me and circle above. I freeze in the center of the soccer field trying to hide my black and white patches. I smell urine. This time I know it's mine. The black bird's screech vibrates the ground, prickles my feet and creeps up my legs until my backbone shudders.

The crows plunge from the sky. "Caw! Caw!" One after the other, they plummet straight down.

My legs will not move. My knees will not bend.

The crows swoop and pounce.

My feet become boulders encased in concrete.

Swish. "Caw! Caw!" they signal, and fly touch-and-goes over my back.

I see hair in their claws as they ascend. It's white and long. It's my hair. I didn't even feel them pull it out. I hold my breath, my muscles freeze. The wind from their wings sweeps strands from my eyes. I cannot manage even a bark.

Whoosh. Their dives continue. Lowering their weapons with me in their sights, they reach down with their claws and grab. A miss. Another dive, swoop, and grab. That one is after my ear. Poop pops out of my rump and piles into a mound like deer scat, and I'm not even squeezing. Another miss. An uncontrollable wail spews from my throat, drowning the sound of the crows.

Elizabeth appears. Thank all the *dogs* among the stars for looking after me and sending my gentle guardian. Dread drains from my muscles. My knees bend. I can breathe. I gasp, chug in some air, choke, and inhale some crow feathers. My muzzle feels like when you eat too much ice cream and your head freezes. Sneezes start and will not stop until the choking starts again. My eyes tear and the birds become a blur. Elizabeth strokes my neck into calmness, but I still feel as confused as a dog with two tails.

The crows seem to stop in mid-flight. They've seen Elizabeth armed with a fresh plastic bag and have become disinclined to continue their attack. One by one they land, perching in the copse of white pine.

I am deliriously happy, but dizzy. I am relieved, yet feel like vomiting. My breathing comes easier as my sobs subside. I lick Elizabeth's hand. I rub against Elizabeth's blue-jeaned leg. I love this woman.

* * *

It's a few suns later and I'm in the back of the car headed for you-know-where, again. We have not seen Spot since the horror. I have paced the carpet bare in Elizabeth's hatchback when I pause to glance out an open window. As I watch trees and cars whoosh by I wonder if I should leap from the window before we get to Ella Sharp Park. Jumping, I sense, would not be the hard part. Landing would.

I choose to take Wolf's advice. "Face your fears," he told me. I wonder if he knew how hard having courage could be? Personally, I'd rather experience a case of intestinal worms. Elizabeth has given no advice, just the direct order. I was to get in the car and together we would get to the bottom of this frightening incident, like it or not. I suppose it's time to grow up. But brute fear weakens my resolve as we arrive at the park.

Elizabeth drags me from the back seat. She attaches my leash and shoves me straight toward the field of bad dreams. I am heeling, touching her left knee by the golf putting range when we bump into Spot with her guardian. Elizabeth suggests they talk. I don't make eye contact with Spot. The woman confesses she has an explanation for the unusual behavior of the birds.

"My Dalmatian is usually a loving pet," she says, "but Spot does not always make good choices. Three weeks ago we were walking in the park when she saw an injured crow under a white pine tree." The women talk while they walk.

I glance over and give the Dalmatian a questioning look. She explains what happened. Her detailed account is as slow as a crawl over broken glass and emotionally as painful.

"I walked over to investigate some feathers on the field," says Spot. "I found this ugly crow lying on the ground." Spot speaks as she looks straight ahead and we walk. "Just for fun, I nudged the body with my nose." She stops to scratch her ear before continuing. "The bird was still alive but smelled great, like rotting flesh." She stops to lift her nose, like she's savoring the memory. She explains that its wing had bent back on itself. The Dalmatian curls her paw to demonstrate before she continues. "The bird flapped the wing that was not twisted, so I grabbed the crow by the good wing and dragged it in the snow. It was so light. That bird flipped this way and flopped that way trying to get away. It almost did."

I look directly into Spot's eyes, an aggressive move for any dog. "You mouthed an injured bird? You dragged a handicapped creature?" My breakfast kibble is curdling in my stomach. This dog has crossed the line.

"That jackdaw was already a goner, Herbie." Her eyes smolder. "Anyway, it couldn't fly. That stupid bird fought me with its beak." Spot shakes her head like she didn't believe what happened next. "It made me so mad I hauled it all the way to the soccer field in the snow. Then another crow flew down and scratched me right here." She stops walking long enough to show me a scab on her hip that has almost healed. I can hear her teeth grinding. "That stupid crow made me so mad." I watch her jaw muscles spasm. "It could have disfigured me."

With her teeth still clenched, she describes the screeching sounds the belligerent black bird made: "Aii, Aii. Caw-caw-caw! It was an awful racket." She wrinkles her nose, squeezes her eyes to slits, and tilts her head back. "Crows look so big and black in the sky but are surprisingly light. I tossed it like a Frisbee. And dumb. That crow was so stupid! I stood there on that soccer field and watched it try to crawl backwards into a snow bank." Spot guffaws. "Birds can't even crawl forward. What a stupid thing to do, should have known it couldn't get away from me."

I am no longer walking. I'm standing with my knees locked, horrified. Didn't this bully know the entire murder of crows must have watched and would retaliate? Didn't she know trouble was ahead when a flock of crows was referred to as a murder of crows? "Spot, are you the daughter of stupid?" I can't swallow. I take a deep breath and focus. Resignation sets in: what has happened, happened. Someone will have to pay.

"So," Spot continues, ignoring my insult. "I jumped around, barking at the crow to keep her from backing away from me. She stopped moving and laid there. So I raced up to the top of the hill, checked my bearings, and with my tail as a rudder, charged down the incline straight for that bloody bird. You should have been there, Herbie. I was great…ran like a greyhound. I pounded past the crow, circled around the field and ran back up the hill for a second pass. This time I hammered down the incline so close to the bird that its black feathers flew in the air. That was some day." She shook her head. "You should have been with me. Herbie? Herbie, you're falling behind. Let's catch up with the ladies."

"Spot, wait!" I say. "I can't listen to any more." My stomach feels like it was kicked. This dog's behavior must be what Calle calls evil. Her brutality makes my stomach cramp.

The Dalmatian falters. "You all right? Herbie?"

I can't answer. I look at my own black and white coat and wonder if spots make every dog evil. I am not all right, and may never be all right. The crows' threatening behavior makes terrible sense. I can't breathe. I sink to the sod and wish Spot would stop barking at me.

To these crows, I am as guilty as this blotchy bully for torturing that poor bird. The park turns and the horizon tips. This Dalmatian and I look the same to the murder of crows. Calle had warned me that bad deeds usually cost a lot. She is right, again. "Did you kill the crow?" I make myself ask.

"No, we had to go home. Probably some lucky cat made the kill and ate it."

This is the first time in my life I want to take a bath. When I'm dry I want to crawl under Elizabeth's geranium-scented sofa pillows and never come out. I want to wash away Spot's scent. I want an endless emptiness of dots and spots on my own coat, and in my life. I manage to stand, turn, and walk quietly toward Elizabeth and the station wagon. I do not like myself.

"Hey, Herbie. Where are you going? Want to race?" Spot says. "Hey Herbie."

I stop and turn towards the Dalmatian, "Don't you feel anything?"

"I think I'm hungry," Spot says.

I remember Calle telling me that anyone can make a poor choice. She said what was important to a dog's life was what he did with what he learned after making the mistake. I take the first step.

"Spot, I don't want to be your friend." I sense I am moving in the right direction because the tightness eases inside my chest. She stares after me as I continue moving away from her, my shadow growing larger as I trot farther from the poor excuse for a dog I have left standing on the turf.

"Herbie, you're soft!" she barks.

TWENTY-FIVE

"I want to learn everything," I say to Calle when Elizabeth and I return to Clark Lake. "I need wisdom."

"That is better news than hearing you brought me a roasted shinbone," the old dog says. "Wolf and I were right in choosing you."

My thin-skinned alpha interrupts our conversation as he steps over us on the patio. He's carrying a small broom which he uses to sweep the rear carpet of his car. He leaves the back door open and returns inside the cottage. "Get out of my way, Herbie," he says on his next trip to the car with a box of papers. "I've got a big day ahead. I'm entertaining some important clients and I don't want to be late."

"Caw! Caw!" I see crows swarming on the sunrise road. Calle watches as I race up the driveway and discover the dead rabbit being picked apart by crows. When they see me approach they fly away. I look at the poor animal. It should be respected in death. It should have a burial instead of being pulled apart.

I'll hide the wabasog carcass from the crows. I'll ask Calle to help me with the ceremony when the black birds have all flown away. But, where can I hide a dead rabbit? Not under the forsythia bush. Not in the hibiscus plant. The crows will find it in the willow tree.

It comes to me in a rush. I pick up the animal and hide it in a place the crows will never think of looking and return to where Calle is waiting.

"Can we start now?" I ask. "What does the name Potawatomi mean?"

"Sit." Her tail is thumping. "This word describes a tribe of people who keep the fires alive. Chippewa, Ojibwa, and the Potawatomi tribes kept their fires burning during the long Michigan winters. They were called the Three Fires Nation. The People shared a common language with tribes living by the great water that tastes of salt which is far beyond the borders of an echo. The language was called Algonquian." Calle stops talking and says, "Walks Like a Bear, never move your lips when you're memorizing names."

"Right." I recall when Elizabeth's furnace failed and the house grew cold. "Calle, Bob restarted our fire when it went out. Are you sure the fires of the People never stopped burning?"

"Natives were skilled at building fires with flint stones or by rubbing dry sticks together. During the cold season the fire kept the family warm in their wigwams. A village fire kept the stew pot simmering all day for anyone who was hungry. Keeping a fire burning could also mean keeping the history of the People alive and burning in our ears, remembering the legends forever like you and I are doing. Welcoming a stranger to the circle of a cooking fire was an act of friendship whether it was sharing a story or a meal."

I scratch my ear with my back paw, signing that I have heard and understand. I tell Calle about the incident with the crows.

Her eyes close to slits. She shakes her head. She is quiet while the sun moves across the sky, only speaking as dusk threatens. "The Potawatomi call the crow Kagageng. Their cleverness is legendary. Rumors are true of crows hiding stolen loot in the crotches of trees, hollow stumps or high up between rocks in outcroppings. They have great memories and can live to be a hundred."

"A hundred winters?" I gasp. "I must make peace with them or I'll be food for them and the buzzards."

"Be mindful you don't become a lido," Calle says.

The way she pronounces the word makes it sound vile. "What is a lido?"

"You will understand when the time is right."

I think I already know one, but I don't tell her it has black spots.

Bob's car careens down the driveway as Calle is leaving the patio. He jumps out, slams the door hard and stomps into the cottage. He looks upset. It occurs to me this may be a good time to hide somewhere. I can hear him inside screaming at Elizabeth.

"There I was dropping my most important clients off after a disastrous appointment at the finest restaurant in Jackson. The house specialty was pan fried rabbit legs, but they all refused to eat a thing at lunch. They didn't want to ride back to their office with me, but I insisted. They hardly said a word. Back at their office building they rushed from the car leaving the doors wide open. The big boss told me he wouldn't make a decision on an upset stomach. He said he wasn't surprised by my sick sense of humor and walked into his building. When I turned around to close the car doors I saw a half-eaten rabbit on the floor.

Elizabeth, how the hell did that dog…where's that book on training dogs? What do you mean you can't find it? Find the backpack and you'll find the book. Isn't that simple enough?"

Laurice LaZebnik

TWENTY-SIX

The crows roosting in my tamarack stalk me. They start by announcing the blazing sunrise at first glow, squawking like farmyard roosters. My sleeps are restless, my eyes swollen. I eat without appetite. I doze and jerk awake, dreading the screech of dawn. The thieving wretches watch what tree I mark and then jostle my message with dung. They watch where I bury bones and pinch them when I'm asleep. They hide my treasures in the crotches of trees where I can see but can't reach. I take to reclining beneath the low limbs of the red cedar or nap under the picnic table away from their prying eyes.

The crows' constant surveillance causes my nose to itch. From where they perch they can swoop down and startle the breath from me, and they do. A twitch develops in my eye. It grows worse as I realize how strong the birds can be. I see a crow steal two cobs of dried corn, fly both to a branch… one with each spidery foot, and pluck kernels off one at a time. Their talons could clamp my spine and rib flesh from my ribs. My knees shudder as I recall seeing crows standing on the north wind road pecking red meat from the pavement. By now both of my eyelids flutter. I am cornered. I must find another channel. Perhaps I could talk with them. Maybe I could get them to agree to a truce. I need help. I need the advice of a wise counselor.

"The People respect crows like they do all creatures," Calle tells me later that day. "The gift of the crow is communication. These black birds have been known to warn when danger approaches."

"How can I respect a bird that hunts me, wants to batter and bash me against the blacktop?"

According to my mentor, the crows that roost in my Tamarack can also squawk good news. "Like the owl, the crow is only a messenger sent by the Great Spirit. Remember this: when you hear the call of a crow, news is coming from somewhere. Pay attention. Smell the wind. Listen to the trees. If you make the effort, crows can be your friends. Walks Like a Bear, what's wrong with your eyes?"

"Oh that…just a nervous tic I get when a crow caws or when I see one perched in a tree."

"I see," Calle says. "So it's not serious." She shakes her head and chews her front paw pads. "It is the custom of the Potawatomi to treat all animals as brothers, even crows. Most animals respect and return this belief. Yes, Walks Like a Bear," Calle answers before I can ask, "Potawatomi hunt deer, fox, beaver, and even the makwa. But, the People would never torture an animal like Spot did with that crow. That is not the path we take."

"How did you…Calle, someone in our neighborhood is killing fish and geese, more than they can eat, and leaving the rest to spoil on the compost pile in their back lot. My Elizabeth is complaining of the smell. Can you imagine that? What could smell better than putrefied fish?"

"It appears this huntsman repeats his mistakes when he kills more than he can eat, and does not learn. He lacks judgment and is not welcome in the circle of my cooking fire." She clears her throat. "Herbie, it is not considered good form to inform on others to divert attention from your mistakes or the poor choice you and the dog with dots made. I heard all about what the Dalmatian did from the crows. To them, your association at the park with the evil one makes you as guilty as she is, even though you didn't hurt the bird. You will never repeat this blunder."

I swallow hard. "Spot and I are no longer friends." I squeeze both eyes tight and clench my teeth. When I open them they still twitch. I must be dishonoring the spirit of Bear. I hate it when that happens. I realize now how close I have come to being excluded from the circle of Red Dog's cooking fire. I change the subject in the center of a long, awkward silence.

"I'm confused. Sometimes you talk about the wisdom of the Potawatomi. Other times you speak of the language of the Algonquin. 'Learn from your elders,' you say. 'Listen to the wind. Watch the stars. Remember the legends.' Is all this wisdom somehow connected?"

Calle smiles broadly exposing yellowed teeth and blackened gums. Her front shoulders slide back to full attention. "That question reflects the wisdom and the spirit of the makwa. I am proud to give this answer to my student. Your eyes can stop twitching."

And they do. I sit up straight, pleased I have pulled myself out of a spiraling, self-destructive tunnel of mistakes.

"We are all one family, you clever sheepdog," she says, pleasure beaming from her watery eyes. "Our wisdom nests in levels of intimacy, like water and family. Think of the Algonquin of the First Nation as the big river of the Elders. The Three Fires Nation as a stream of the parents. The Potawatomi tribes are the lakes of the cousins. The stars and wind are the creeks of the sisters and brothers. The family you live with is the pond of the child. You and I, well, think of us as two dogs in a puddle, banded together. We could be washed away in the night." Then she says, "That last part is a joke."

I smile. "Calle, I feel like I'm knee high in muck standing in our little puddle trying to figure out how to work upstream toward home. That is a joke, too." We both laugh.

"It's not simple, Walks Like a Bear."

"You may have to explain that last part to me again, and again." I remind Calle that yesterday she told me the part of the legend where Mennaboju made a new world after the wicked snakes killed his pet wolf pup and flooded the world. I have a few questions. "Can all snakes swim?"

"These did and assumed Mennaboju drowned." Calle scratches her ear with her back paw, licks the front of her leg, and pauses, looking off into the distance like something's wrong. "I hate it when I forget why I'm barking. I'm old, Walks Like a Bear. I must hurry."

"You were telling me what happened to the snakes…how they were hiding on the bottom."

"You listen well," Calle says. "Now I remember. When the snakes noticed the newly created islands, forests, rivers, and prairies, they began to doubt their success in destroying Mennaboju. 'Perhaps he is hunting and enjoying life while many of our own people are still laid up with the wounds from his arrows.' The arrows Mennaboju used were magic arrows dipped in a secret poison. Wounds inflicted by them healed slowly."

"Were these the arrows tipped in ground frog livers?"

Calle stops abruptly and shifts her gaze to me. "How did you know about the frog livers? That is privileged information and should not be widely known."

I look away, slumping to make a smaller target. "You don't remember, but you were the one who told me. You didn't say it was a secret, but I can keep it secret."

"That would be wise," she says. Her tone softens as she continues the legend. "During a snake council some cunning turtles, *mishike*, advised the snakes to make ropes out of twisted reeds and twigs. They were to spread them like a net over the entire world, but tie one end of the rope to a mishike's leg. Mennaboju was bound to bump into one of the ropes when he went hunting. The mishike on guard would feel the tug and report the location. All snakes agreed to the plan and set out to twist as much rope from reeds and twigs as was necessary to cover the whole world with a net."

Calle rearranges herself on the straw. She smells good, like rancid pork fat. Her bones creak like they could crack open and deliver out their marrow. The Irish setter excuses herself for the day. She's exhausted, but pauses before she curls into her sleep ball. "Herbie, a man has been standing at the end of your driveway. You haven't seen him because he hides behind the pin oak. He's watching something in your yard. I've seen him several times. He has heavy black hair on his arms."

I back from Calle's wigwam and walk home around the narrow path by the lake wondering why a man would be stalking me. I listen for that hissing sound, that cascade of sand that comes just before the ice water sweeps a dog into the night. Perhaps his target is that bug-eyed ice cream-sucking Bob. I fall asleep with a broad smile on my face.

TWENTY-SEVEN

We work it out. I guard the northern conifer while the crows sleep. They put off pecking my eyes out. I let them steal seeds from our bird feeders. They agree to keep confidential my treasury of treats. I provide reparations…dog biscuits discreetly hidden among seawall rocks, yet clearly visible from the air or the Tamarack where the crows perch. In exchange, they offer hope that I will see another sunrise. That is the deal.

"You're feeding Herbie too much!" The man with the shinny hide on his head who calls himself my alpha bangs the counter with his fist. "How much do you give him, five pounds a week?" He stations himself before the kitchen sink, and while rinsing his breakfast dishes sneezes and wipes his nose on his sleeve. "He'll get sick." The boiled egg-sucking old coot wipes his watery eyes with the back of his hand and loads his dishes inside the dishwasher. He grabs my chin hair, pulls my face next to his and says, "You. I'm talking about you, lard bottom."

This man fires insults at me like it's a bodily function. I stare into his eyes. "Let go of me. I'm warning you. Stand back. I have several contagious diseases, too."

He drops my face and takes Elizabeth's plate from her hand. "I'll have to pay higher vet bills if he gains any more weight." He places her bowl in the dishwasher, picks up loose change from the counter, and puts it into his pocket. "Can't you see how fat he's getting?" He reaches down and while he's rubbing my belly, sneezes again. He runs his hands from my withers to my rump, his hands absorbing every lump. "I feel layers of fat, not ribs."

"Herbie knows not to overeat, unlike some grown men I know." I see Elizabeth wink at Bob. "My sweet bean buries his excess for later, like squirrels bury nuts for winter," she says. "I've watched him. He buries all kinds of things in the garden and the seawall. He's like you. You bury M & M's under the cushion of your green leather chair. I've watched you, too."

"Elizabeth, he buries the biscuits because he has too much to eat." The man with the unbridled brain sneezes again. "Elizabeth I feel as sick as a dog."

Is that supposed to be some kind of insult? I growl to vent my anger, but my grumble is soft so Bob won't hear. I may look vulnerable to him…like I don't understand his verbal abuse, but I'm just practicing temper control. I'm fully equipped to take revenge on my own terms. I happened to see him pee on his own foot once. And another time I saw him puke on Elizabeth's roses. I'll never forget either event, and I won't respond to his probes. If Bob wants to cut my ration and put me on a diet, a measure that would violate my parole and endanger my life, I'll deal with it. I can understand why the birds are blackmailing me, but I don't understand why this man my parents have entrusted me to is making my life so unpleasant. Bob stays on my back like a bad case of mange.

I steal into the pantry while they're watching television, clamp the knob of the bi-fold door with my teeth, pull, and then push each flap wide enough for a clear shot at the cookie barrel. It takes a couple of tries before the lid pops and I've grabbed a mouthful of dog biscuits. I nose the lid back in place, push the flap closed, and hide the cookies under the rug by the front door. When Elizabeth lets me out to move my bowels, my job continues as the crows' cookie courier.

If Bob still has a stuffed nose and takes to his bed after sunset tonight he won't know what irregular practices occur in his home each night. He won't smell wet dog in his chair. He won't know how many cookies are missing from the closet barrel or how many are buried under the cushion in his chair or in the back pack in the garden…petty offenses. The one who must be obeyed may never learn who pulls the spread off his bed.

TWENTY-EIGHT

"You want me to repeat the entire story?"

"Yes, Mrs. Hartman. It's standard procedure to vet the facts."

"Okay Officer Diesel, I'll tell you what happened, but I've already told the whole story to the other young officer," says Elizabeth. "I was awakened by Herbie's bark and then by his growl. Herbie is my sheepdog. I'm a sound sleeper so I didn't hear anyone break into the cottage. But I must have heard something because when I sat up in bed someone pushed me down or fell on top of me…I don't remember which…it all happened so fast. I reached up and felt a hairy arm…and that's when I heard a man's voice cry out. Herbie, my dog, was breathing heavily and growling like he does when we play tug-of-war. I heard a rip, like cloth was being torn. The man skidded off me or was pulled off me and thumped hard on the floor. He took my blanket and the top sheet with him.

"I was confused and still half asleep. I got up and flipped on the lights. By this time the man and Herbie were in the hall or the kitchen. My blanket was on the hall floor. I picked it up to cover myself. The light fixture over the fireplace isn't too bright and there was no moon that night, so I couldn't see well. I did notice a dark smear on the bottom sheet. I knew the sheet was clean when I went to bed. The bottom of my slipper was dark with an oily pool of blood.

"I heard shouting and growling and thumping from the kitchen…like pans were being jerked from the counters. I heard them clatter on the floor tile. Then I heard glass break.

"I flipped the light switch for the lake room and saw the back of a man as he pulled the front door open and limped outside. One of his legs was bare to the knee. Both his arms were bare and covered with dark hair. Herbie barked and followed him to the door, but didn't step outside. My dog was loud. I usually don't let him bark, but this time I wanted him to wake the neighbors. He stood there barking and together we watched this person disappear up the driveway." Elizabeth gives me a pat on my head. "A short time later Herbie walked back into the bedroom…like the ruckus was over and it was time to go back to bed. While I called 911 he curled into a ball in the corner and stayed there, right where you see him now."

"Did you see what the intruder looked like? Was he tall, thin, overweight? Did he have dark hair, light hair, long hair or short hair? Was he wearing glasses? Are you sure it was a man?" says Officer Diesel.

"I saw his profile, but can't describe him. The light was dim and he was wearing dark clothing. And yes, the prowler was a man. He had to be with all that hair I felt on his arm."

"Did he speak to you? Would you recognize his voice?"

"No and no."

"Did you see where he was in the house, how he entered? Is anything missing? Did you feel you were in danger?"

"No. I told you I'm a sound sleeper and didn't hear when he entered. I didn't think about danger. I was too groggy. Nothing is missing."

"Except for one of my slippers, the dog muzzle we ordered, most of the dog biscuits from the pantry closet, my baseball glove and hat, and that dog training book," Bob says. "Oh, and the backpack."

"Get serious Bob. You know you misplace things all the time."

"Excuse me, Mrs. Hartman," Officer Diesel says. "I need to speak to the detective." I can hear Officer Diesel ask someone to make a plaster mold of the shoe prints in the snow and the tire track in the mud and get a sample of the blood to be analyzed. "Have you seen a torn piece of pant leg in the house anywhere? We need to check it for skin or hair to sample for DNA. Do you have a security system with a camera, Mrs. Hartman?"

"No."

"Has your dog ever bitten anyone before?"

"No."

"May I check him for evidence?"

"Of course. He wasn't injured, but had blood covering his chest and paws before you arrived. Hold on, officer. I'll just tell him you're one of the good guys." Elizabeth kneels beside me and strokes my back. "It's okay, officer. Herbie will cooperate."

I hear Officer Diesel's knee-bones crack as he squats. "Will Herbie let me touch his front paw without biting me?" Before Elizabeth can answer I present my paw. "He's pretty smart," says Diesel.

"He seems to know what I want even before I ask," says Elizabeth. "I know this sounds crazy, but I think he reads minds."

"Is it okay if I pull out my flash light so I can see his paw better?" says Officer Diesel. "I don't want him to bite me?"

This is the kind of policeman stray dogs like. When the long tube emerges from his belt, I hear a click and a light comes on. He waits until I turn my paw over, squints and tilts his head.

"He's used his claws on the intruder, Mrs. Hartman. One toenail is broken." The officer flashes his light over my chest. "There's some blood here. The intruder must have some serious wounds. We'll check the hospitals and clinics. Your floor is bloody. We found a trail of it up the driveway and down the road." Officer Diesel gets to his feet.

I offer the evidence I have torn from the intruder.

"Well, thank you, Herbie," he says, leaning down and taking the bloody pant leg from my mouth. "You are quite a dog. First you save your mistress' life and then you save me work." He laughs and turns to Elizabeth. "I'll bet five bucks your dog will be the one who solves this case. I hope you know this is an amazing animal."

Elizabeth smiles, "I think so and now maybe my husband will think so too. Do you suppose the intruder will come back?"

"This doesn't look like an average B & E to me. We haven't established a motive for his being here...you say he hasn't taken anything. The man seems to have known your husband was out of town. His big mistake was underestimating your dog. If the guy comes back your dog will recognize his scent. I doubt you will ever see him again."

"We're done out here for now," says the detective from the lake room. "We'll come back in the daylight to scout the area for anything we missed tonight."

"That should do it for tonight, ma'am," says Officer Diesel. "You can turn your outside lights out. We secured your front door. Lock everything and go to sleep. You'll be safe with Herbie until your husband gets home. He doesn't look like a mean dog, but I see he can be vicious if he needs to protect you. He'd make a good police dog...does his job and goes to sleep. And that's just what I'm going to do, Mrs. Hartman. Good night."

TWENTY-NINE

Elizabeth has an unpredictable look...high, broad forehead, a long nose, luminescent fair skin and narrow lips, a tall beauty...not like a woman who could heat up a head of steam, move fast, and catch me relieving myself on one of Bob's shoes. I understand now that I am not to do that again. My nose still stings.

Out in the kitchen I watch as she moves the sweet smelling bowl from the counter to the cloth covered table. I have been warned off this table, too. The cream has a fragile, poignant flavor and smooth texture, but I don't have time for more than a taste before her eyes catch me.

I don't know if I hear the broom and then see the flash, or if it is the other way around. It is an awful smack. I lie on the kitchen floor, open-mouthed from the pain, and watch the liver she fries arc up into the air and fall back into the pan. Not one piece drops to the floor for me to taste. She hears me gasp, bows with pride and sets the meat to cool high up on the window sill. The smell is irresistible. I wonder if…

"Outside, Herbie," she says. "Bob will be home for lunch soon. I've cleaned his shoe, but if he catches you…"

Okay, okay. She's reading my mind more and more these days. I exit the kitchen door she holds open and find a spot in the sun for a nap. I try to grab a small piece of sunlight, but it slips between my paws. I wonder if Elizabeth realizes how much pleasure I give her each day. I wonder if she understands it's not the dog in her life, but the life in her dog that makes her feel good.

It's so good to have a decent scratch on a patch of skin that's been eating me. I don't mean a burr that's poking or a bug that's biting, but a hard to reach itch that's been here since dawn. It takes some time until my paws pass over the exact spot, but now I'm in the throes of ecstasy. My eyes are rolling in my skull. I'm experiencing pure joy.

My hard-skulled alpha has been hanging around the house more since the break-in. Elizabeth tells him she's fine and for him not to worry about her, but I watch her walking around during the night, checking the door locks and gazing out windows. If she spends any time outside when the sun is out she's jumpy. I go with her to mail a letter, collect the newspaper from the roadside box, or track the army of ants advancing on our house.

Sometimes Bob walks me in his pajamas before the sun wakes, his hair a tangle of serpents. Sometimes we walk after dusk when he comes home from work. I prefer walking with Elizabeth. She lets me sniff neighborhood news on message trees. When I'm with her she hooks me to a long leash so I can study squirrel trails, deer tracks, and raccoon scratchings. I've taken to patrolling the entrance to the driveway while she's digging in the garden. One sound from her and I'll be at her side. I'm always on duty.

A disruption in the west wind rattles my meditation. The honk-a-honking of a wildfowl shakes me from my thoughts. A black and white gander glides low, flares his wings and stalls, skimming the lake just off my shoreline. His feet are a lurid orange, like tiger lilies. The flappers are flat like paddles and hang from his under frame. Dragging them creates a wake which splashes onto my seawall.

His flight plan changes; his webbed-feet cup the water, scuttle faster and faster until he is aloft and the orange paddles retract. The gander accelerates over the tree line, glides gracefully and drops from view on the far side of Clark Lake.

I have memorized the distinctive stamps on this goose: black head and neck, white chinstraps and gray-brown plumage…easily distinguishable from other migrating waterfowl. I enjoy identifying birds that rest on our lake during their journey north: the great blue heron, the bufflehead, the northern pintail, and the common loon. The mallard and wood duck hang around the lake all winter. Recalling waterfowl that deep in my bird chain makes my eyelids heavy, my mouth stretch into a deep yawn and my breathing slow to a rumble. I am almost asleep when cold water sprays over the seawall again, startling me awake. Wind created by this Canada gooses' sudden landing blows my hair back flat against my head.

He flaps his wings to propel him from the water, and settles on my seawall…uninvited. You would think that on a lake as long as ours, this edge-stepper would choose another landing beach. This piece of shoreline is the only place I get decent sleep.

The honker drops his leavings on my lawn and with no apology, heads straight for me. Wildly annoyed, I step aside to give him room to stagger by, but the loathsome bird stops on the spot I have warmed in the snow and scoops up kernels of popped corn I am saving for my snack. "Where are his manners?" I wonder. "What is he doing here? Why isn't he flying with his own kind?" I scratch my ear, curious about the interloper but still angry enough to dispatch him with a warning growl.

What saves him is his excrement. His leavings are long and lean with distinctive wild bird scents: sea grasses, weed seeds, cracked corn and algae. These choice sausage shaped crisps crunch when I eat them.

The goose flaps his great wings creating a flurry of blowing snow. He puffs his feathers and hisses. His long neck snakes around to a weary head buried beneath one wing. The old gatecrasher is quiet, at last.

What an imposition! He knew what he was doing when he took my spot. His white under-tail won't get cold now. I could threaten the feathered freak, frighten him or push him into the lake, but my memory of the crow's capacity for carnage is still raw in my mind.

I decide to ask him to move south when his flock arrives… nicely, with courtesy and respect. I recall Beau's warning. "Do not corner something that you know is meaner than you." My annoyance level downgrades to one of tolerance. I feel weak in the loins.

THIRTY

Calle stumbles into my yard not long after the bird's dramatic entrance. It has been almost a moon since I last visited her wigwam.

"Thanks for the cookie. Where'd you get it?"

"The alpha has a new hiding spot by the back door."

"Did he catch you stealing treats?" she says. "Thought so." I nod toward a place on the snow and she sits beside me. "Nice goose. Friend of yours?" She breathes in the aroma of fresh excrement. "You saving these leavings?"

"Help yourself."

"Ever try deer scat? Scrumptious. Buffalo chips? Crunchy with a wild edge. Elk dung? Delectable. Horse manure? Marvelous."

"No."

"Emm. I heard the commotion over here the other night."

"Did you smell that stranger in my yard?"

"How could I miss with the stench of human blood? Was that your work?"

"Calle, the man's scent was familiar, but he's not been in our yard before. He may be the man you warned me about."

"You sound tired," Calle says and swallows the goose leavings, still fresh and soft. "Want me to ask the bird to leave?"

"No, don't! If he powers up those wings again we could both be blown into the lake. Will you finish that story you started when the moon was full, the one about the end of the world?"

"I've forgotten where we were in the story," Calle says. "Are you sure you want to talk about this now, with all the excitement at your house?"

"It's okay. Takes my mind off what I don't understand. Before you fell asleep you told me that in the beginning when all animals were friends of the Great Spirit, he was hungry and went hunting with some wolves. You called him Mennaboju, right?"

"Good job, Herbie," Calle says, "but a legend is only as good as its details. Remember names, dates, and if you expect me to laugh, try to recall the punch lines to your jokes."

"Right." I scratch my ear. "You told me that Mennaboju adopted one of the wolf pups as his pet." I'm showing off my memory now. "When the pup strayed out on the ice-covered lake, Mennaboju's old enemy, the snake king, reached up and pulled him under. That night at their camp the snake king threw the carcass into the stew pot. Later he enjoyed the tender puppy-stew for dinner."

"Well done, Herbie. How much more of the legend do you remember?"

I scratch my ear. "Mennaboju wanted revenge, so he waited inside a hollow tree next to the family campsite until the snakes had fallen asleep. That's when you went to sleep, too. And, that's all I can remember."

Calle gulps down the last of the excrement. "Haven't had anything this good all season." She licks her lips. "Okay. Here's what happened. When all the snakes were asleep the Great Spirit slipped out of the tree trunk, found his bow hidden under a bush and dipped his arrows in frog gut poison.

He shot every one of them and threw their corpses into a tree top."

Unraveling from Calle, I plead with her to change the story. "It's too rough for a dog my age. Violence gives me bad dreams."

"Herbie, this is a legend. A dog cannot change a story that has been passed down for generations. Come back," she says and pats the ground. "I'm still cold."

As Calle and I watch, the sleeping goose uncoils his neck from beneath his wing. He stands, stretches, and wobbles forward on his wide webbed feet. Both of us grow silent and watch as the gander pauses to move his bowels in place and then waddles toward shore. He clambers over the seawall stones, slips, and bumps down the rock barrier on his tail, overturning on the lake ice. He lands with his tail pointing skyward.

A howl bursts from my chest, although I attempt to control my mirth.

Calle gives me a stern look. "Herbie, show some respect."

"But Calle, this is the goose I saw glide into a faultless soft landing. His touchdown was acrobatic perfection, liver candy for the eye. He didn't stir a single snowflake. I'm laughing because no flock would want him to fly in their formation if they saw him maneuver on land. This goose must be an embarrassment to his peers. No wonder he's alone."

"Herbie," Calle says. "Think. Geese fly in pairs. Perhaps this gander is looking for his mate. She may have been shot or she may have contracted a disease. There is a reason he is not with his flock. Think with your heart."

The gander rights himself, shakes off the loose snow and lumbers toward the open water near the artesian well. His awkward orange feet leave a trail of prints toeing out. He steps into a small hollow of open water, spins and pumps his feet, thrusting his breast against the edge of the ice.

"What's he doing?" I say to Calle.

The large bird forces the rim around the open water to crack, chip and break away. Time after time he churns the water and pushes, whittling a hole large enough to float comfortably in a pool of open water. This clumsy waterfowl has returned to a picture of power and majesty. When I can force my eyes from the bird, I say to Calle, "You have been calling me Herbie lately."

"What?" Calle says. She is still mesmerized by the grace of the goose.

"You used my Potawatomi name before. Why are you calling me Herbie now?"

She turns her head. "When you don't think before you speak, you are undeserving of your First Nation name."

Calle's displeasure feels like a flogging. I bow my head, nod, and lodge my nose in the red fur along her back. Chattering like a chipmunk is crude, I know, but if I try thinking before I speak, it will slow conversation to a crawl. "Calle, does every creature deserve courtesy…even Bob, that conceited slush-head?"

"Even Bob."

"But he's so nasty to me, and he smells revolting, like laundry soap." We watch as his VW pulls into the driveway. The alpha steps out. A vulture perched in the hickory nut tree arches its red featherless neck and flies away. "Bob stinks worse than a sun soaked corpse by the side of the road. Did you see that? He almost made that vulture sick." Bob walks toward the cottage hiding a bunch of fresh flowers behind his back. "He must be in trouble with Elizabeth."

"Is he top dog in your pack?"

I nod.

"There is your answer. You must respect his position. If he offends you, he may have a reason, and he may not. You hear the things he says, but you don't hear what he doesn't say. Look beyond what is obvious."

"Why not just tell me to swallow the sun?"

"Herbie, it is possible if you try. Do you recall how much that Canada goose annoyed you?"

I think about ignoring Bob like I do the goose as we both watch Elizabeth open the front door and wrap her arms around her husband. She doesn't seem to mind his odor. He kisses her. They go inside and close the door.

"Emm." I scratch my ear. "Calle, do you suppose Bob could break the ice with his big stomach?"

"Herbie." Calle smiles and scratches her ear. "Just try to be kind," she says and continues with the legend. "Mennaboju discovered three more snakes, and without saying bojo, he riddled all three with arrows."

"That's it!" I say and jump up, fully recovered from my reprimand. "Why can't the Great Spirit find another channel, make peace with the snakes instead of killing them? I would chase Mennaboju and those snakes into the forest if it would stop them from hurting one another."

"Never intervene in a disagreement, Herbie. Both sides will bite you." Calle pats the snow again. "Now, take your place here beside me."

"Okay. Okay," I say. My own bones creak from the cold as I bend towards the ground.

"Harmful behavior surrounds us every day," the red dog explains. "You are too big and too old to hide under Elizabeth's bed when thunder cracks. Some may look at you as potentially dangerous because of your size. All that hair makes you look huge. Don't act like that goose. Don't intentionally annoy others. Walk away from that kind of behavior. Your road is to use your strong heart to find a path around anger that is not destructive, to use your strength without cruelty. Remember what I have told you. You will understand why when the time is right."

My gut is in a knot. I have enough questions to fill every waxed slide in the honey bee hive, but I want to hear the rest of the legend, so I clamp my jaws together, and nod for Calle to continue.

"The snake has an ability like no other to shed his skin in order to grow," the old dog says, "to move ahead leaving his bad behavior behind. Think of the snake as a symbol of growth, and of gaining wisdom by learning from mistakes." Calle's voice trails off, muffled by a gust of wind.

I can hear Bob happily cursing from his chair inside the cottage. He's watching a game on the TV. I wonder if that stranger will come back to hurt Elizabeth. I wonder if the Great Spirit would have killed those snakes if they had already shed their skins and changed their life style. I know a man with a bad attitude who sheds his gray hair all over the shower floor and he still has a bad attitude. I wonder if all that hair Elizabeth combs from my coat each night is making me wiser.

You were wondering again, says Wolf.

"Hello Wolf. Got any snake stories?"

Sure. Will you listen and remember them?

I scratch my ear with my back paw. "*Forever, right?*"

Longer than that. This legend is about a snake shaman who escaped the killing.

"Great! I like this snake. What's a shaman?"

…he's a smart snake with great powers, like your Doctor Hauschild. He fixes what is broken, and sometimes breaks what must later be fixed by someone else. So, this shaman snake slithered into the lake and whipped the water with his long tail. He

sprinkled charms from his medicine bag and blew powder into the wind. The water rose and circled in muddy swirls. The sky covered over with storm clouds. Torrential rains soaked the land. Mennaboju's neighborhood was flooded. The water got higher and higher until half the earth was swamped. It wasn't long before the whole world was covered with water.

"Stop the story," I tell Wolf. "I changed my mind. I've had my belly full of all this violence." Questions pour out of me like an unblocked ice flow. "Why must people die? Why should animals die? Why kill the grass and trees? If each of my brothers die, why would I want to live? How can a snake face his brothers knowing he will be responsible for all this?"

Walks Like a Bear, no raindrop forming a flood ever feels responsible.

"But, Wolf, don't snakes think and feel? Don't snakes love? Don't snakes bleed?"

Of course they do. They care just like you and Calle. But there are some, my friend, who are so filled with hate, some who fight with such passion to win that it makes no difference to them if their kind survives or if the earth is destroyed. No life is sacred to these barbarians.

"I don't want these creatures in my world."

I told you, Herbie, you cannot change the story. Accept it. Evil will always be here. The spirit of the bear inside your heart can stop it.

"Why couldn't they…how would I…oh, I give up. It's too hard. I don't want to do this…"

The spirit inside you will speak when the time is right. Listen to your heart, my friend.

Calle stirs from her sleep and shakes her head. "I must have nodded off. Where am I?"

"Herbie, it's time to go." Elizabeth pulls on her gloves as she approaches the pin oak and announces, "You can keep me company while I run some errands."

"Are you serious?" I bark and back away from her. "The world is lost and you want me to help you with errands?"

"I think someone needs a nap," Elizabeth says, grabs my collar and tugs. She stops moving when a gust of swirling snow surrounds us. "Your new friend must be afraid of me," she shouts as the Canada goose flaps his wings, stretches his neck tall and takes off into the wind. My guardian brushes the snow from her shoulders and watches the bird until it crests the trees at Eagle's Nest. "Isn't that a wonderful bird?"

No.

"Herbie, sweetheart, let's go. I have some cookies for you in the car."

I blow off steam inside my cheek. "All right, I'm coming," I say, remembering to show respect for those I don't understand. I grumble all the way across the winter lawn. "That old goose blew me awake too early."

"Walks Like a Bear." It's Calle. I turn to see her stumbling stiff-legged toward her fence. "Remember to keep a soongetcha, a strong heart, like the makwa that you are."

I watch her faltering steps as Elizabeth drags and pushes me up into the hatchback. I can hear Calle's moans and the creak of her bones as she makes it around the end of the fence, along the honeysuckle stalks, and up the hill to her wigwam. I curl into a ball while the car backs up the driveway and dream ways of ending all this violence. I sink into a deep sleep. When I open my eyes we're home.

Back inside the cottage Bob glances up from the newspaper. "Herbie went nuts on our walk this morning," he tells Elizabeth. He takes the glass of wine she offers. "He saw a beggar leaning on a cane, growled and tried to jump him. I thought he was going to tear the guy apart. It was all I could do to hold him back with the leash. Another guy that jogged past our house a week ago had the same effect on Herbie. I forgot to tell you about him. He was about the same height and was wearing a cheap leather jacket. He may be a neighbor, or… will you call that detective so I can talk to him?"

"Officer Diesel stopped by yesterday," Elizabeth says as she sets a plate of chopped chicken livers down for my dinner. "He said no medical facility in the area has reported treating a man for dog bite to his leg, and no B & E's in the area since ours. It's a mystery. I'll call the detective after dinner."

"You give that dog chicken liver? You don't give me chicken liver."

"We eat in five minutes."

"I'll walk the moth-magnet until they catch the guy, which better be soon. All this exercise isn't good for me."

"Thank you, honey, but I think you're wrong…about the exercise." She sets placemats and silverware on the dining table and disappears into the kitchen. "That jogger is a complete puzzle to me, too." She places bowls of hot food on the mats. Bob finishes his wine with one hand and pulls out her chair with the other.

I gaze up at my guardians happily chatting about the news of the day, enjoying each other's company, laughing and eating something green. Before me is one of the humans in my world that I love the most, and the other is beginning to grow on me.

When I look up I notice a small, perky, roasted chicken crowning each of their dinner plates. My mouth starts to water. I think I would love roasted chicken. I wonder if…

THIRTY-ONE

I snap awake when the horny owl hoots. It's dark. Trouble threatens the air. I can feel it in my spine. I can't open my eyes, can't move my head. I wonder if I'm alive.

In a short time I feel the warmth of my old friend the sun dancing along my spine. My under-jaw whiskers are stuck. I remember falling asleep under the pin oak. My beard, stained brown and smelling of mildew, must have frozen to this pillow of snow. One quick but painful jerk and my chin rips free.

At least I can move my head. My eyelids, frozen shut in the night, should not be an obstacle to my daily routine. I know this yard like I know the folds in my paw.

A few steps past the edge of the patio I'm blasted by a blizzard sent howling by a Southwester. I follow the throat of the wind to the lakeside passage, and like a blind dog crossing a busy street, feel my way around the fence, along the honeysuckle and up the hill to Calle's wigwam.

"Bojo, Walks Like a Bear," I hear the Irish setter say. Her voice is louder than her normal growl and pitched higher to be heard above the gale. "Come inside."

Something sounds odd about the way my learned friend is walking. She clops irregularly instead of stepping lightly with her familiar rhythmic clip. It's like she's moving with her paws turned in. She told me once Potawatomi women sometimes walk that rhythm when they carry heavy loads.

Calle's peculiar shuffle stops and starts. I can't see what she's carrying but it must be heavy.

"Come close today so we can stay warm. I'll tell you how the earth was found."

I could use some good news. I stagger to what I remember being my assigned place and fall to the floor in a heap.

Calle catches her foot on my bulk and stumbles. "Stop that dancing you crazy animal," she says. "There's no room for such foolishness inside my wigwam."

"Sorry, but my eyes…." I recall Calle telling me she didn't want to hear excuses. "I apologize." Spoon-curling around the old dog, I throw one leg over her spine to give her the benefit of my belly-warmth. I sniff the floor of her wigwam for what she was carrying but find nothing extra but straw. She's still shivering. I float my long hair over her arthritic haunches and tuck my nose along her neck. She smells good, like the damp potato bin under the O'Rileys' house.

When we have wiggled and grunted ourselves comfortable, I remind her where we are in the legend. Mennaboju is holding to the tallest tree on top the tallest mountain and attempting to persuade animals to swim down and collect soil to restart the world. So far the loon has died. The muskrat is next to feed the buzzards unless he refuses the Great Spirit's request. "I can't imagine volunteering for a job like that," I tell Calle.

"Someday you may need to retell this legend, pass it along as an example to answer another's question. Your task is to keep the history alive. The Great Spirit almost gave up hope, like you did when you contemplated jumping from Elizabeth's car. Yes, I know about that. Wolf told me. You must never lose hope, Walks Like a Bear, never. Do you understand?"

"Never give up on hope. I've got it," I say, and hope this ice will melt and I will be able to see again. I'm anxious to hear what happens next in the legend, so I don't mention my loss of sight.

Her head is at the center of our two-body coil. Calle whispers the legend. "On the day after the muskrat agreed to dive, Mennaboju saw its limp corpse floating toward him in the waves. He caught hold and blew life into its mouth. When the rodent could breathe easily, the Great Spirit said, 'Brother Rat, we're both in deep trouble if someone doesn't find the earth. I need you to dive down into the water again. This time bring me some soil...even if it's only a little bit. Even if you only bring three grains of sand, I will be able to make something from it.'"

"Calle, that muskrat already died once."

She ignores me. "The obliging muskrat dives, but shortly after bobs back to the surface…dead."

"I've got to keep track of this. That's twice for the muskrat and once for the loon. Okay, let the violence resume. I hate this story."

"No matter, remember it just the same. The muskrat floated on the water as he had before. Mennaboju caught his little body and examined its feet. In one of the small front paws he found a few grains of sand, dried them in the sun and blew them across the water using the magic of his breath."

"Was the dirt the muskrat had in his paw like the dirtballs I get between my paw pads? Is that what killed him?" I licked my feet and sucked the dirt from between my toes. "I don't want to die because I have dirty feet. Could that happen to me?"

"Walks Like a Bear, listen to the legend. See what mistakes were made. You can learn without having to make the same mistakes yourself. Remember, this is only a story. Your destiny is determined by your decisions, not legends. Understand?"

I scowl, and scratch my ear to sign I have heard and understood. Then I scratch ice from the hair around my eye socket. My sight begins to return. I paw the remaining slush from my face. I'm not blind after all. Calle's body heat gave me back my sight. I'm so glad I didn't give up hope.

"What counts is that the world is saved," Calle says, inspecting my face for the first time under this sun. "What happened to your beard? Did you lose it in a fight with the goose? Catch it in Elizabeth's vacuum cleaner? You look off balance. Tilt your head to the left…a little more. Yes, that's better. Can you hold it that way? Practice, it makes all the difference in your appearance." Calle gestures her approval, and rests her head on her paws.

"What happened to the muskrat? Did he stay dead this time? How about the snakes? Did they shed their skins and begin a new life, or did they finally give up their war?"

Calle scratches her neck with her back paw. "This patch of skin is eating me." She tries to reach the spot with her front paw and fails. She clears her throat. "Herbie, I'm having trouble remembering. Come back with the morning sun." Her eyes look sick and match the color of her coat. "It feels so good to scratch an itch."

"Umm, rest now," I say, uncurling from my mentor. I nose soft straw against her old spine, inch my way from her wigwam and step into the deep snow. I shuffle around the fence and along the seawall, careful not to crack the ice and fall in like the wolf pup, the white-tailed buck or like I did earlier this moon. At the compost pile I nose under the frozen layer of angleworms and stuff in another boot I pulled from Bob's closet this morning.

THIRTY-TWO

Watching the power of the dawn makes my knees weak. I think the sun expects me to be on this lawn, at this cottage, on this lake waiting for its message. I feel like I belong to this land. I belong like a tiny bead belongs sewn into a buckskin legging by a Native American woman. Calle's descriptions of The People are etched in my mind.

I wonder if people from the First Nation chose colors from the sunrise or from trees to paint their bodies. Calle told me body markings were used to give warriors courage before battle. Colors chosen had to be fierce to scare enemies into fleeing instead of fighting. I imagine myself as a warrior's dog with a black stripe down my spine and slashes of red paint on my jowls. I would look fearsome and feel brave. I could wear eagle feathers if I made a kill and touched my quarry, or accomplished a great deed. The trouble is I don't want to kill anything, even a bug in battle. I'll find another way to decorate my coat. I wonder why eagle feathers are such a big deal.

Walks Like a Bear, you were wondering again.

"Oh, hello Wolf. *When Eagle takes to the sky above our lake I have noticed a peculiar scent fills the air which sends small animals and birds scurrying. All the time Eagle circles the scent is strong and creatures hide. Eagle frightens them into silence. This bird must be evil. The bird scares me.*"

Walks Like A Bear! Do not insult Eagle. When Eagle flies so you can see him, it means he has a message for you. His meaning is for you to stretch your limits, to be more than you are or thought you could be, to grow.

"Why do all the birds hide deep inside the trees when they see Eagle fly? Why do rabbits dive down their holes if they are not afraid?"

If Eagle scares or attacks you it means there are some self-imposed limitations you will need to push past.

"The only limitations the mallard duck or the silver bass had were they didn't smell the danger scent soon enough or swim fast enough. Eagle grabbed them and flew off."

Walks Like a Bear, Eagle doesn't fly. Eagle soars. When he comes from the direction of the dawn, the message is to start over again. If you are having a hard time, sighting an eagle can make you strong enough to endure the bad time. If you see Eagle, you can soar like he does.

"Hmm."

I know what you're thinking. No. Don't try flying. Eagle simply means he wants you to think, to expand your view. And when you find a feather from Eagle and qualify to wear it, the message is you hold a small piece of Eagle's greatness in your heart. But then you must take on the responsibilities and power of Eagle.

"Herbie's been rolling in the compost again." Bob's voice tumbles over the lawn to where I lay dreaming with Wolf. "He's a mess. I've been picking leaves from the kitchen floor all morning. See that!" Bob stands with his hands on his hips. "He's getting into the ferns now. Elizabeth, I swear I'm going to get rid of all the plants and trees in this yard and pave it so that dog won't drag his mess into the house." He tramps to where I am relaxing. "Get off that pile of twigs, Herbie." He leans down. "Get into the house."

I jump to my feet and shake my coat clean.

"Now!"

When Bob howls my heartbeat increases and I have to pee, no matter where I am. This demanding alpha must have inherited his carload of courage. I leave puddles in the grass as I dash to the front door. The man will never understand what it takes to strengthen a dog's heart. When I first came to Clark Lake I had no idea courage took this long to grow, to bud, and then to blossom.

Later, when the sun is highest, I hear a knock on our door and smell Officer Diesel.

"Mrs. Hartman," he says. "Our detectives picked up the intruder, the same man your dog recognized last week. The guy jogged by your house this morning. The stakeout your husband suggested worked. When we checked on this fellow we found he had some priors: assault and battery and bank robbery. He was recently divorced. The guy has a history of robbing ATM's."

Elizabeth's head tilts and her mouth drops open.

When he bumped into you in the grocery store, he must have recognized you from one of the banks around town. He glances around the room and finds me under the table. "Oh, there you are, Herbie. You certainly are the hero of this case. Mr. Hartman, this is one smart animal. If you ever want to sell him, give me a call."

"Last week I would have given him to you, but not this week," Bob winks at Elizabeth. "I'll keep him around for another day or two."

"Do you happen to have an identical twin?" the officer says to Elizabeth.

"No she doesn't," Bob says. "This guy sounds like a nut case. He assaulted my wife. What will happen to him?"

"He didn't hurt me," Elizabeth says. "He just scared me a little. Did his wife divorce him while he was in prison?"

"Yes, and she was the one responsible for his incarceration. The man was in your bedroom Mrs. Hartman. In our interview after the incident you did say you were scared. That counts as an assault."

"Don't I have to identify him? Don't you need some sort of proof, Officer Diesel?"

"Yes, you can identify him from a photo if it would upset you to see him in person. He is outside in my car."

"I'll see the man now," she says.

Officer Diesel nods and opens the front door for Elizabeth. As she approaches the vehicle she leans her head to one side and looks in a window. "It's not him. I can see that from here."

"Are you certain?" says the officer. "Take a good look."

"I thought you said it was so dark you couldn't identify him," Bob says.

"I changed my mind."

"Well, I guess that's that. We will release him."

"Thanks for all you've done," Elizabeth says.

"Have a nice day," he says and his car backs up the driveway.

"It was him. Tell me the truth," Bob says.

"I didn't see his face. It was dark that night. I can't send anyone to prison. He didn't hurt me. Herbie hurt him. Besides, wasn't that a terrible thing for a wife to do? I wonder what he did to her to make her so angry."

THIRTY-THREE

"Calle, why don't I see families of the First Nation when I walk in the forests by Clark Lake?"

"The People and their animals were moved far away. The pioneers took their lands."

"Why couldn't they share?"

"It's complicated," she says. She pats the ground beside her. "White settlers cleared the forests and farmed the native's unbounded land. Wild animals were over-hunted by the white squatters. The Potawatomi needed to buy their food at supermarkets like Elizabeth does because fresh meat was scarce. Without wild game, the natives had no furs to trade or meat to eat."

I lay down beside her to hear the legend I would remember forever.

"Settlers resented the natives hunting among their settlements which had been built on Native American land. They sold whiskey to the natives and then complained when drunken warriors threatened their homes. Complaints were decided by local white officials. The men asked the white government to remove the brown-skinned people."

I shrug. I tire of disputes based on the spots or colors of coats. Most dogs I know think Spot has a mean streak, but not every dog with spots kills crows. Not every black dog bites children. Not all men who wear caps with bills like ducks kick dogs. Any canine adopted into a home knows every female is not as caring as Elizabeth. My mentor told me the legends teach us that every creature that breathes must choose his path. "Calle, didn't any of the pioneers get along with The People?"

"Most white settlers around Clark Lake were afraid of the natives because of the news that Indian raids were killing the early settlers in other parts of the land. One exception occurred the winter of the great blizzard.

"The Hitt family lived in a log cabin by Clark Lake not far from the Bear Clan's village. The wind was cold and the air was damp that winter. Times were hard for Barks at Birds tribe. Food was scarce, the snow was deep and the tribe was hungry. While ice fishing, the Potawatomi could smell beef stewing on young Mrs. Hitt's wood stove. The native custom of sharing led the natives to ask her for food. She was alone with her children during the day so naturally she was afraid the first time they visited.

"They looked different from white families living around Jackson. Many native women carried cradleboards with their papooses strapped to their backs and wore calico dresses. Most braves wore buckskin leggings and brightly colored flannel shirts. Both wore beaded moccasins and covered themselves with striped trading blankets. Some of the braves wore eagle feathers woven into their hair.

"It didn't take long for Mrs. Hitt to see the People of the First Nation were only hungry and meant her no harm. The youthful woman served them stew and shared whatever extra food she had stored in her cellar. The People came back often during the blizzards that year. After that stormy season the Potawatomi were always kind to the Hitt family and welcomed them to the circle of their campfire. They shared fresh game with the Hitts and introduced them to rose hip tea to prevent a disease called scurvy.

"Native Americans were naturally suspicious about the growing number of settlers moving onto their hunting and fishing grounds. They were puzzled by the whites' strange customs. The path from the village to the lake came close to the Hitt's log cabin. During the day curious Potawatomi braves with their dogs looked in the open windows as Mrs. Hitt worked. It made her nervous. When two of her children grew ill and died from a coughing disease, she convinced her husband to move away from the lake for the health of their family. The couple built a house at the top of the hill, away from the damp lakeside cabin. Members of the Hitt family still live in that house today.

"The life of the Clark Lake Potawatomi changed forever the day Barks at Birds watched the tribe's pups play in a bay a few yards from where my wigwam now stands," says Calle. "Barks at Birds had taken the small pups from the village to teach them how to swim like the turtles. They played one-stone, two-stone, red-stone, blue-stone…a noisy game. They splashed water on each other, laughed and jumped between canoes resting along the shore. That's why they didn't hear the tumult. When they returned to their village at sunset, wigwams were empty, cooking fires cold.

"At first the puppies looked for familiar odors in their own wigwams. They chased scent trails into the field of ripe maize left standing in the snow. They looked for them in the river where the natives bathed in the winter, in the mounds where the food stores were buried. Nothing had been disturbed. Tired and hungry, they returned to camp, lay in a pack by the cold fire pit, and howled into the night.

"Many suns later they overheard a conversation in the Hitt house that explained their clan's disappearance. The Potawatomi and animals of their village had been gathered by the *Kitchimokomans*, the long knives.

"The white soldiers found most of the clan eating in their wigwams when the sun was highest in the sky. They were given little time to round up their possessions. Having no knowledge of where they were being taken, they left the village quickly and were forced to march to an encampment on land towards the setting sun on what was called the Sauk Valley Indian Trail.

"For the young and very old it was a hard trek. One hundred-fifty natives tramped for two suns. They camped in open fields southwest of Clark Lake near a town now called Pittsford. Their home for over a season was near the St. Joseph River where they met other Potawatomi clans.

"Together they fished and hunted within a fenced area they were forbidden to leave. The braves trained and raced ponies for many moons. They repaired their war and hunting equipment. The women cut saplings to make wigwams and burned the brush clearing small plots of land for farming. They tilled ash into the soil, planted corn, squash and sunflowers in mounds fertilizing them with fish from the river. The fenced growing fields supplied most of the food for the large encampment, but the reservation was a prison to the native people.

"The night her village was abandoned Barks at Birds found a large deerskin bag of pemmican and a relic at the entrance of Chief BauBee's wigwam. The relic was part of the Chief's official headdress, a feather from the kiniou, the eagle. Barks at Birds was convinced it was left as a reminder for her to keep a soongetcha, a strong heart.

"Instinctively the young dog knew the puppies could not stay in the village. She took the kiniou feather and with her pack hid in a cave in the woods beyond their former encampment. The sole movement seen outside their cave for many sleeps was a wavering column of smoke rising in the quiet night air. It came from the Hitt family's new house on the north wind road.

"Soon all the pemmican was gone. Since Barks at Birds knew she was incompetent as a hunter, she led her little band of refugees to the Hitt farmhouse and claimed their doorstep. The pups whined and pleaded for scraps of food. The good-hearted mistress recognized them from their visits with the Potawatomi and gave the panhandlers meat stew, bones and warm milk.

"The pups played with their children. Barks at Birds found comfort with the Hitts. The dog that had been cast out by the Potawatomi hunters found his life's work. Barks at Birds, with his pack of pups, protected the Hitt family from that day onward.

"Barks at Birds died a few seasons later of old age, but not before she told the pups the legends of their elders, the story of their history. They promised to pass the stories along to the next generation. This was the way of the People, and so it was the way of the animals of the People. Barks at Birds chose Night Sky as Keeper of the Legends when it was her time to be reduced to dust. Night Sky chose Basket Dog who chose Spirit Walker. Each dog of each layer of living was special right down to the dogs that carry on the tradition today. They all promised to pass along the legends and a kiniou feather to the next generation."

This is how Calle finishes her story. She stretches her mouth long. When her yawn subsides she invites me to return when the sun slides toward the skyline. Red Dog excuses herself and is asleep before I can agree. My mentor looks sick and smells worse than Bob's boots.

On the way home I pause near the lake to clean my paws. Basket Dog may have stepped where my toe just touched. The soil tastes ordinary and smells of fish. I pass the craggy rock where the cyclone fence stops. Spirit Walker may have marked this lakeside anchor. Her scent may have washed away but her stories continue.

I am beginning to see how this legend business works. I sniff the granite crag, inhale Calle's scent, Beau Schmidt's, mine, and, what the...what is the odor of Bob's urine doing on this boulder? Could he be marking the boundaries of his territory?

THIRTY-FOUR

"Herbie! Come!" Bob barks. "It's time to eat."

Today is like every day, my belly rules my mind. I scoot inside thinking...that man is a shiver looking for a spine to crawl up. But then my next thought pops...What? Dry kibble, again?

Elizabeth and I go for our afternoon walk. Since her old backpack can't be found, I wear a new backpack that looks like the old one. It's stuffed with even more heavy books and is held with another pair of red suspenders.

We take the same route for the next three days. On the fourth day, a rope gets caught around my neck and a foul-smelling rag is held to my nose. The next thing I know I'm in a crate in a damp, night-soaked room that smells moldy like a cellar. Could this be a show on television and could I be dreaming?

This is my short list of questions: Am I supposed to be a bad dog or a good dog in this basement bin? Will I get fed when the action is over? When does the action start? This cellar smells real.

I stand to stretch and notice I'm not alone. I catch Elizabeth's scent. She's on the floor near my crate. I paw the wire and whimper to get her attention. "This is no time for you to take a nap," I whine. She moans. I can hear her move. "Elizabeth," I bark.

"Herbie?"

I hear her gag, hurl, and say, "I'm all right now. Ether always makes me sick."

The smell of vomit isn't my favorite. I gag but manage to hold my digested food in place. I hear her moving around the space. She bumps my crate.

"Just a minute, Herbie. I'll try to get you out."

I escaped from a crate like this when I was a younger. This should be easy.

Elizabeth tugs and pushes and finally resorts to kicking the crate in the darkness. "I can't do this, Herbie."

I recall a number of disassembly moves in succession. The wire box folds flat, so it's a matter of finding the clips that hold each side together. The ends fold in first. I feel with my nose along the top edges.

"I can't see the damn clasp. I'm sorry," she says.

Metal holds human scent. I sniff and locate the scent of musk, a stench some men leave with their hands. I pull the clip with my paw while I push the end panel with my chest. The wire frame moves. The gate bangs when it hits the floor. I crawl out before the crate collapses, avoid Elizabeth's stomach fluids and locate my guardian leaning against a wall. I lick her face and clean her ear. She's okay. She laughs and pushes my head away.

"How did you do that, Herbie? You are so clever." She rubs my ears. "What happened to us? Where are we?"

I pace the outer wall of the room. It smells wet and moldy. A snippet of fresh air pulses from above me, tempting my nose to sneeze. I edge up the wall and smell old wood. Stretching, I find a loose corner in some molding and nudge it open with my nose. A beam of afternoon sunlight exposes the basement room. A blink later Elizabeth is at my side. She pulls the remaining molding and cardboard from the window.

"Herbie, we're below ground. It's some sort of basement," she whispers. "If I break the window pane we may be able to squeeze out." She glances around the bare room. "I need something to stand on." She pauses. I see her smile. "I'll reassemble that crate. You look for a rock…something to break the glass." She begins setting the crate upright as I search the room.

I hear footsteps approaching on a distant sidewalk. I spy a shelf near the ceiling filled with cans, jars, and boxes, and nudge a long-handled mop with my nose. The wooden handle skids along the wall and thumps into something made from glass. A large glass jar with brushes hits the concrete, and shatters. A foul-smelling liquid spills out on the floor. The shelf bounces from its bracket and falls. Cans and jars scatter across the room. I carry a roll of tape and push a heavy can toward Elizabeth.

"Herbie, you're a genius. Of course I'll need to tape the window before I break it. We don't want the sound of shattering glass to give us away." She tugs the crate under the window, climbs on top, tapes the window and taps it with the heavy can.

I barely hear it crack, but I do hear the footsteps and they're getting closer. Elizabeth taps the top edge of the glass until the pane falls outward into the window well.

"Herbie," she whispers. "Someone's coming." She removes the broken glass held in one sheet by the tape and sets it to one side. "Can you jump up here beside me. I'll need to stand on your back to get out of this window well."

"The crate looks too flimsy for both of us," I whine. The footsteps are louder and sound like they're moving down a staircase.

"Hurry Herbie," she whispers.

I stand on my back legs and put my muzzle flat against the wall.

"I'm sorry but I'll have to stand on your head," she says. "Here I go."

I squeeze my eyes shut. Of all days to have a headache. My skull is crushing. Elizabeth never looked this heavy at home. Her foot pushes the headache down into my jaw and out into my nose which seems about to burst.

"One, two, three," she whispers and the weight is gone. I hear a grunt, and then a, "Damn. I'm caught on something."

I'm experiencing a vacuum from the loss of pain when the basement door is flung open flooding the stairwell with light. The flash of light blinds me, but spotlights the scene behind me...Elizabeth's butt stuck in the window-well. The silhouette of a man fills the bright arch. His dark arm moves to one side of the door and a light bulb hanging from the ceiling blinks bright. He stands at the top of the stairs with both his hands squeezed into fists.

"Let go of me!"

I see a hairy arm and his two hands on Elizabeth's leg.

"Ouch! You're hurting me!" she screams.

I attempt a rush, but the hair along my nape gets caught. I'm thrown to the ground. The man stands over us both now stretched out on the floor. His legs are spread like twin tree trunks. His hairy hands slap his hips. His scowl cuts a slice between his eyes. "Where's the money?" he says. He sounds threatening, but I sense he's acting. The villain is a small man and looks like a perfectly pleasant sort of person in silhouette, a curly headed, mustached man bundled in a knit sweater, hat and scarf. When I squint to see into the light I see he's the man that stood in line in front of us at the bank robbery, the man Bob calls the ATM thief.

"What are you talking about? What money?" Elizabeth says. "Where are we? Why are we here? Are you the man the police picked up in my neighborhood? Who are you? Why did you pull me down on this floor? Are you going to hurt me?" Elizabeth's voice is remarkably calm considering she was just caught with her butt stuck in a window well. I wish for once she would stop talking and listen.

"What did you do with the bank cards?" The man seems almost friendly.

"I went Christmas shopping. What do you think?"

He lowers his voice. "You think you're clever?"

If he could understand me I would say to this man, "Life would be simpler, mister, if you would walk around the bee hive. Even a clever dognapper shouldn't try to mess with my Elizabeth. Trust me."

She laughs. I think she read my mind.

"Let's go." He extends a hand to help her up.

I growl and gnash my teeth.

He backs away. "I've got this new gun I'm aching to try out," he says. "I need a target." He fingers the trigger. "You seem like a good dog. I'd hate to kill you."

"You seem a good fellow," I growl. "I'd hate to die."

Elizabeth rolls to her knees and stands. "Save your bullets. Herbie will act with restraint, won't you Herbie?

I scratch my ear with my back paw. She understands, and the man does too.

"That's the sign for 'I understand' isn't it?" he says.

This guy is literate in Native American sign language? Nice. He'll have lots of time to scratch his ears in jail.

"Let's go," he says and draws a gun from his belt. "Your next hideout won't be this nice. It won't have a window and both of you will be down there until the money arrives." He sounds mighty serious.

Elizabeth heads up the stairs and out the door with me by her left knee. He follows with his gun pointed at her. When we reach his car he opens the trunk.

"Get in," he says to me. "Just the dog," he tells Elizabeth, pushes some tools aside and picks up a roll of duct tape.

"Herbie honey, jump into this trunk or the big bully will use his gun on you." She pats the floor of the trunk with the flat of her hand.

I don't want to, but her eyes tell me to jump. I'm entertaining crippling reservations about our future when I hear the lid snap shut. It's dark in here. I don't like being enclosed like this. I hear a car door slam, and another, and then the engine roars. The motor purrs and I feel the car surge ahead. As my eyes grow accustomed to the dark I investigate the trunk.

The odor is strong, like the new red cooler Bob uses to keep his sodas cold. There's enough room to stand or lie down but not enough for a long stretch. The trunk floor is lined with a material my feet can grip as the car rocks from side to side. The walls are hard and covered with the same lining as the floor. I am thrown to one side and fall. Heavy hand tools rap me in the ribs.

A blink later the vehicle skids to a stop. My head bangs into the wall that separates me from the back seat. I recognize Elizabeth's scent on the other side. Another heavy tool slams

177

into a center panel and pops it open. I get to my feet as the engine roars ahead and stick my muzzle into the hole.

Elizabeth is lying on the seat. Her feet are bound. Her wrists are taped together behind her back. I push but the hole isn't large enough to force myself inside the car, yet I sense this opening may lead to our escape.

Elizabeth sees my muzzle, struggles into a sitting position and covers the hole with her back. She blocks my light. I feel something move, sniff and feel her hands on my face. I lick the sticky tape that doesn't belong on her smooth skin. I pull and chew. She wiggles her wrists. It takes a while but I finally rip off the tape. When her hands disappear the light shines through the hole again. I can see her pulling duct tape from her ankles.

Elizabeth grabs a tool that has slid through the panel, and swats the driver alongside his head. The man slumps, the car swerves, bumps over a curb and slows to a stop in a field.

I thump my head on the lid, land on my side and skid to the front of the trunk where I bang my head harder. My paw gets stuck. It's caught in a crevice. When I wiggle and push my paw the lid creaks open. I crawl out and stagger around the car to find Elizabeth.

The window on the side door looks crinkled but still holds firm in its frame. I can barely see her slumped against the back door. I smell blood. The driver is standing beside the car rubbing his curly hair. He stoops and picks up his cap, then opens the back door.

Elizabeth is leaning her bloody face on the opposite cracked window. I jump in and hear the door slam behind me.

The man zips his sweater as he walks around the car and then slips behind the wheel. One of his arms slides over the back of the seat. The heat from his eyes burns mine. He smoothes his black mustache flat to his cheek. "You will be sorry you hit me with that tire iron, missy. I won't be so nice to you next time."

As he backs from the field, over a curb and onto the road I lay across Elizabeth to keep her limp body from bouncing to the floor.

THIRTY-FIVE

Elizabeth will be sick again when she wakes, if she wakes. She hasn't moved since she bopped the kidnapper with the tire iron. I saw him hold something to her nose, the same rag he's tying around my neck. It smells like strong medicine, the same scent that put me to sleep before. I paw at it, chew on it, scratch at it, but it won't come loose. I remember feeling the hair along the man's arm before I hear the pitch of a stone hitting Elizabeth's garden shovel…the odor in this cloth… the sound of gravel being pitched in the air…so tired…small stones splashing on the ground. Sleep. Elizabeth?

When I wake it's dark. I catch Elizabeth's scent and breathe easier, but I'll admit I'm confused and scared. Her head is next to mine. We are in a cave, or a basement, or a crate of some kind. The walls smell like the heavy cardboard box I found behind the garage.

I investigate. When I lean out and stretch with my muzzle I can touch both sides. It's dark. "Elizabeth, wake up," I whine and crawl to lick her face. I can barely stand. I smell feet at the far end of the carton. When I push my shoulder against the sidewall it doesn't budge. I hear a trickle of sand seeping from someplace above. I push my skull against the ceiling. A solid lump of soil falls on Elizabeth. I push up on the lid again. More dirt. "Elizabeth. Wake up. We seem to be buried." My guardian doesn't respond.

As I wait for her to wake I recall a legend about a Native American brave who was buried before his time. He lived to tell his story and so can we. I lick Elizabeth's face and nudge her with my nose.

"Herbie? Is that..where are…" She gags, turns her head and vomits.

I place my paw on her forehead. She spits sand, coughs and stops talking. I hear her hands rubbing the sides and top of the carton that holds us prisoner.

"This is a coffin," she blubbers between gasps.

I lick salty tears from her cheek until she's calm, then lift her hand with my muzzle and push it against the hole in the lid where the sand is now pouring in. It smells bad in here. I could use some fresh air.

"Are you trying to tell me something, Herbie?" she says.

Elizabeth, it's too stuffy to speak inside this box, just think the words to me.

Okay, boy. I understand. She coughs.

"*Good girl. I know how to get out of here,*" I think to her.

Yes, I understand the weakest point in this casket is on the top of the box in the center where the sand is pouring in. You think that's our escape route? She coughs again. *Yes, I can hear you scraping the soil to your end of the coffin. I can do that too. Yes Herbie, I am scared. No Herbie, I won't panic and I'm done crying.*

I tug the tails of her blouse up until they are wrapped over her head. She understands and pulls her shirttails tight, and ties them under her chin. I retrace my crawl and kick the top of our burial vault like I saw a donkey do on television.

Before long Elizabeth is kicking the weakest spot in the center top along with me. I'm so proud of her quick mind. I feel the dirt pour from the hole we have made. I scratch sand to my end of our box with my back feet and pack it tight, all the time thinking how lucky I am to live with such a clever woman. As the hole expands and more earth pours in I clear it to my corner. I can hear Elizabeth scrape sand to her end. She seems to know we don't have much air left, or extra storage for sand.

We crouch in the center...my nose to her nose. Elizabeth wiggles and bumps and produces a pair of her panties. She hooks them over my head. Before I can think instructions to her she jams my muzzle into the hole. Before I can react her hands are under my rump and she is shoving me straight up from the coffin, up into the sand.

My headache returns with the pressure, crushing my skull, my eyes, and my tender nose. It's a good thing I'm wearing her panties to prevent abrasion. The soil is loose like gravel, and I can feel each stone as it skids by.

The pressure is gone. I can move my head freely. I must be above the surface. I shake her panties loose and fill my chest with fresh air. Elizabeth is still below me, pushing. She's under my rump.

This is one strong woman. When my back legs clear the surface I jump from her hands and shake. I see her forearms. Her head breaches the ground next and I can hear her spitting sand. She coughs. Part of her blouse is still tied around her head. She rips it off and shakes sand from her hair. As I dig her out Elizabeth gasps for air. She brushes loose particles from her eyes.

Soil shoots between my back legs. When my digging uncovers her shoulders, she grabs my head and kisses my nose.

I stop to think…*I love this woman*, and then continue digging. She pulls herself up with her arms, and wiggles and worms her way out. We both lay back. She's coughing between her laughter.

"We did it, Herbie. We escaped from being buried alive."

I hear a car motor. It stops nearby. I hear a door open.

THIRTY-SIX

My mentor told me once how to avoid trouble. She said when the wind kicks up the scent of danger and other animals and birds hide, that's an ideal time for a dog to beat it, too.

Calle said when I see my guardian staring down at me with her hands on her hips and a frown on her face, that's means it's time to hide.

When a wooden outbuilding with holes chewed in its foundation gets re-sided with a long strip of shining metal, and a new hole is chewed through the bare metal, and the hole is large enough for a groundhog, a raccoon, a skunk or all three to crawl through…danger is ahead for any animal light-headed enough to stick his nose inside.

If a larger dog is about to set his fangs on my neck unless I apologize, and instead of a real apology I say, "I'm sorry you're such a nincompoop," that's a good time to scoot.

When I see a swan swimming close to shore and I want to give chase and see if her wings are as wide as Bob says… don't. Those wings are weapons that can break a leg or send a dog on the path to the afterworld with one swat.

When I hear a car approach on a lonely road after surviving being buried alive, and I hear a door open, it's time to run faster than a Southwester blows.

THIRTY-SEVEN

Elizabeth sits upright. "Herbie, is that the same car that…"

It sounds like trouble. I stand and sniff the air, then pull her pant leg until she stands. We sprint towards a stand of trees. Elizabeth is first to dive under a bush at the base of a cedar sapling. I'm right behind her but land in a dark pool of shade near a hollow stump.

We can barely see the figure walking toward what was to be our grave. I do see the scarf he's wearing flapping in the wind. He's carrying something over his shoulder…a shovel. He begins to dig.

"We've got to get out of here," Elizabeth whispers. She picks her way under a branch and around a tree without making a sound. "It won't take him long to reach the empty box." She steps over a log and follows a deer path into the brush. The mercies of moonlight soften the night giving her an otherworldly grace. "I'm exhausted, Herbie. Let's rest." Elizabeth kneels at the base of a tree and curls into a ball.

I scratch leaves from the forest floor and push them over her feet. A fallen branch is light enough to pull over and hide my already sleeping guardian. I crawl into her nest and curl around her back. I wake to the caw of a crow and the sun streaming yellow light through the branches above us. I see the black bird perched near the top of the tree. *Follow me*, it caws. *It's a new day and it's time to move.*

When I uncurl from Elizabeth's back, she wakes. We move through the forest for some time before Elizabeth stops and calls out, "Herbie, you're standing on a hornet's nest!"

She's right. They are hornets, angry hornets, angry swarming hornets. I leap over a bush and keep speeding until I'm beside a pond. The bees swirl above me and dive.

Remember the legends and follow me, the crow caws.

A legend about a young brave who dove into a lake to avoid being stung comes to mind. The swarm in the story circled until the brave came up for air and then stung him so many times he died. I need to avoid the pond and find shelter.

Calle told me hornets can't fly fast and fly even slower upwind. I hear a splash, turn into the wind and run leaving Elizabeth somewhere behind me. Across a large field mowed flat I see the crow circling a building with an open door. I may be able to outmaneuver the swarm.

I avoid the onslaught by turning in circles, racing for the building and dashing inside. I hasten down a hall and into a steamy room filled with laughter.

Young girls scream when they see me and hold towels over their wet bodies. A small female walks over, lets me smell her hand and says, "What's a nice dog like you doing in a place like this?" I'm suddenly surrounded. The girls all pet me at once. It occurs to me that Elizabeth is not hear when I hear her faint voice.

"Herbie?" I hear her call from the hall. "Herbie?"

I hurry to greet her and find her slumped in the hallway, soaking wet, her face swollen and red. The locker room girls are not far behind.

"Someone call for an ambulance," the small female commands. "What happened to her?"

Elizabeth laughs and shakes her head. "Hornets. Allergic." Her lips are swollen so much her speech is garbled. "This is my gog. Will you kee Herkee kets home who Kark Cake."

THIRTY-EIGHT

It's been two suns since Elizabeth came home from the hospital. Bob won't let her out of his sight. Officer Diesel has taken up residence with us and brought my backpack back. I hear them jabbering from under the table where I lay. They are attempting to connect the man who invaded our cottage with the man who hid us in the basement with the man who buried us in the cardboard box. That he is also the ATM robber they don't know for sure. Their supposing this and suspecting that is driving me stone, cold, nuts. I walk to the door and bark to get out of the house and communicate with someone about something else…anything else.

I remember the sun edging closer to the horizon on my way to Red Dog's wigwam. I settle near Calle's door and must have fallen asleep because my next recollection is of Calle waking me with a shake. The sky is overcast and dim.

"Walks Like a Bear," the Irish setter says. "You may as well come in. I can't sleep with you snoring outside my door. You're louder than a pack of Potawatomi puppies."

I stretch my spine into a curve, reverse into a slump and step inside her wigwam. I curl into my usual place and avert my eyes. I try waiting for her to open the conversation, but my impatience gets the best of me. "Calle, how did an Irish setter like you get mixed up with the Potawatomi, the People of the First Nation?"

The old dog moves a thin birch bark bundle with her muzzle and tucks it under her brisket. She clears her throat with a hack, coughs and spits out mucus. "My pedigree goes back to the noble Irish setter breed, but I was whelped in a village called Detroit and moved to Clark Lake as a pup. Blue chose me when she had only thirteen winters. Blue descended from a long line of Clark Lake dogs: Spirit Walker, Basket Dog, Night Sky, and Barks at Birds. I was told the legends of the Elders before Blue went to live among the stars."

The old dog pulls straw with her paws and stuffs it under each elbow, now bare of fur and raw. Her smell is staggering… a mysterious blending of rotting scents: feces, dirty hair, and mold.

"Walks Like a Bear," she says to me, her tone serious. "Elders deserve great respect. Their wisdom is the key to the legends. Legends are the means of change. Change is the solution to surviving. It is my responsibility to share my wisdom with a dog of the next generation so the history will not be lost." She looks me squarely in the eyes. "Walks Like a Bear, I choose you."

"What? Calle, you're spoofing me." I say and look into her eyes. "Do you mean me, Herbie from Ken-Bear's kennel, Herbie who still belongs to the Hartman pack after Elizabeth and I were almost killed?" I look behind me and out the door to see if another animal is standing there. "You can't mean me. I'm a mistake. Where I go trouble follows. I am a bad omen like the owl in the sycamore tree. Elizabeth just got out of the hospital and now won't leave the cottage. Bob takes me on walks so no one will jump me and drag me away and bury me again. Everybody is afraid at our house."

"Are you afraid?"

"No, but I am confused. Do you remember the legend when the Potawatomi woman gets lost and thinks her way home?"

"I may have forgotten that one. Sorry."

"If I could understand why that man was stalking Elizabeth…do you remember the man you warned me about? The one that was watching us from the end of our driveway? You said he had dark hair on his arms."

"No, I don't remember. Do you think he could be stalking me?"

"If I could understand why that man broke into our cottage and jumped on her bed…do you remember me telling you about that?"

"No, I don't recall your telling me that, but that man could have been in the wrong house. He could have been after me."

"If I could figure out who drugged us and locked us in the basement…do you remember me telling you about that?"

"No. I'm sorry, Herbie. I'm worried somebody is after me, trying to kill me."

"I wonder if it could have been the same person who buried us in that cardboard box while we were asleep. He used the same medicine with the putrid scent that made Elizabeth puke. I remember he stuffed that same cloth over my muzzle both times I unexpectedly fell asleep. Calle, the trouble with Elizabeth started when we were at the bank." I look over and see Calle sleeping.

"I'm not sleeping," she says. "I'm listening with my eyes closed."

"Good idea. I'll close mine while I wonder what happened at the bank that was different than all our other trips to pull the green papers from the wall? The police came. I smelled gun powder…that was different. Elizabeth pulled some green papers from the machine, but not nearly as many as the man standing in front of us. He was the man who pushed Elizabeth up against the wall and put his knee on top of my backpack. I thought he was scared like the rest of us and was trying to find a place to hide. Maybe he was the one the police said they caught but let go because they didn't find any green papers in his pockets. I wonder if there could be a connection. I wonder where his papers are?"

Walks Like a Bear, I heard you wondering.

"Calle, Wolf is back." I paw her side but she doesn't move. "Hello Wolf, are you still watching over me?"

I told you I would. If you could remember forever like you promised, you wouldn't have to keep asking me the same questions. Walks Like a Bear, are you still wearing your backpack when you go walking with Bob?

"No."

Why?

"I buried both of them in the garden."

Didn't Elizabeth ask you to wear them weighted down with heavy books to strengthen your legs so you could someday participate in dog shows?

"The first one was too heavy. The second backpack was even heavier. Both are with the tulips. And now the crows are digging in that garden."

Crows? What else did you have in the backpack pockets besides the heavy books? What would the crows want in the flower garden?

"Calle, are you sleeping or listening?" I shake her again.

Red Dog doesn't need to know. Tell me.

"I had a few bones in the back pack. That's all, just the bones and those books. Wolf, I don't want to be a show dog. It's too hard. Elizabeth wants me to lug those books around while I'm training. I don't want anyone to know about the bones. I buried them deep so animals wouldn't find them."

I drop my head in embarrassment. "Wolf, I lied to Elizabeth so she would still love me. I lied to Bob so he wouldn't take me out into the country and leave me. I lied to Calle so she would never find out I haven't remembered all the legends she told me. I can't lie to you. Wolf, I am a thief and a coward. Isn't there a legend that will show me which channel to take? Or should I bury the lies like Elizabeth and I were buried, and like I buried the backpack in the garden?"

By now you should know which channel is right. You have heard enough legends. Bojo, Walks Like a Bear.

"Wolf, don't go? Wolf?" Sadly, I do know what to do. Tears flow from my eyes as I dig the black soil. I find the back packs in the garden. I can't make myself open the flap of the one buried first to see all those delicious bones I know I must give up. I carry the canvas bags to our front door and place them on the patio. This may be my last trip to Calle's house. When Bob finds out I stole the bones he will take me to the dog pound and Elizabeth won't be able to save me. I stroll back to Calle's wigwam and hear her snoring. I wonder who would want to hurt Calle.

THIRTY-NINE

"Walks Like a Bear?" Calle says after I cough to get her attention. I have been waiting outside her door for some time. The old dog blinks sleep from her eyes and continues, "Where were we? I might have nodded off. What were we talking about?"

"Calle, you said you chose me to be Keeper of the Legends, but your memory is not as gifted as it once was and I think you have me confused with another animal. It's me...Herbie, your friend from over the fence."

"I know you are the one like I know there will be a morning sun." She rubs her nose with both paws, and settles into the straw. "You were in the dream of my youth."

"Calle, are you certain you have the right dream?" I ask. "I've only seen half a season at Clark Lake."

"It is true you continue to learn about survival. It is also true that you ask extremely feeble questions, come to unbelievably stupid conclusions, and continue to get into incredibly burdensome troubles. Walks Like a Bear, every one of us that has a life filled with adventure gets into trouble sooner or later."

"I make the most dangerous mistakes of any animal that marks the history trees, more blunders than all other animals combined, and much louder trouble than even Bob can create. You may want to revisit this decision after you get some fresh air. Go outside and smell the trees. The odor in your wigwam might be clouding your judgment. Besides, I'm not sure this is what my sire had in mind for me when he said he expected greatness from me."

"Herbie, fate is determined by what a dog learns from making mistakes, and by the changes he makes in his behavior. Each of us can change our lives, and change the lives of others around us by how we act. Don't look so confused. Yes, you can be a very foolish dog." Calle is laughing now. "There were times, my young friend, when I was convinced you were channeling to be a chucklehead." She scratches her ear. "But you have shown that you can learn and are capable of change. You will survive to carry the legend, and when the time comes, you will pass it on to an animal of the next generation."

My mind is dizzy with the responsibility that comes with a little knowledge. What happens if I mix up the Elders' legends? My foot starts tapping and won't stop. I sit on it so Calle won't see how anxious I have become.

"Calle, what will you do if I become Keeper of the Legend?"

"I'll stop eating and die."

"Calle…"

"Herbie, before you grind out another thought, just look at it from my viewpoint. Why should I prolong my pain? We all must die someday, and since I have already made such fine strides in that direction, I have no desire to turn around now only to start again another time. So I am refusing kibble and waiting for the end. Anyway, I must make room for others the way others have made room for me. No more food, thank you."

"So you mean to starve yourself into extinction? That sounds like the worst kind of pain any dog could experience." I say.

"It is a little uncomfortable, especially when my guardian offers me chopped chicken liver and ice cream. Look at it this way. After death, either we feel better or we feel nothing."

I am quiet for a long time considering our futures. I wonder how long Calle can live without food. I wonder if she will change her mind if she gets hungry enough. I wonder if I can live up to her expectations. I wonder how I can exist without my mentor. I wonder why Red Dog chose me, an Old English sheepdog from next door who has barked impatiently and rudely these many dawns, an admitted coward, a bone and cookie thief. I wonder why the crows were digging in the garden. Were they telling me something?

"Calle, I still think you've made a grave mistake…trusting me to pass on all that knowledge. You're getting old, you sleep a lot and maybe…"

"I still have a few moves in me, Herbie." She cackles before her tone dives back deep into a serious strain. "You are not alone thinking that you know so little. The longer I live the more I think and inquire and the less I seem to know. Try to be just, compassionate, and humble. That's enough."

So there it is. Me, the neighborhood poster dog for bad behavior; me, the pup with the defective coat that could never be a champion; me, the last to be picked at our kennel, now chosen to carry the legends…one of the most important jobs in our kingdom. I jump in the air and roll on my curly sunburned hair. "Does Wolf know?" I ask as uncertainty raises its ugly head again. "Hold on, Calle. I didn't say yes, yet. Maybe…I don't know, but maybe."

"Walks Like a Bear," Calle says. "You have not only brightened my chain of life, but added lengths to it. Will you promise to live a life to honor the spirit inside you and to pass on the legend when it is your time?"

"Yes, Calle. Yes, of course I will. You have my word," I say with friendship in my heart.

"Then to you I give a feather from the kiniou, not the same one, but an eagle feather like the one worn on the heads of great warriors. Guard it, Walks Like a Bear. It is part of the old to give strength to the new. Now go. I am tired and nearing the bottom of the hill," her voice trails off to a whisper.

"Bojo, Calle," I say to the fading hound, taking the delicate feather surrounded by fluff that once adorned an eagle's tail. I refold it into its protective birch bark wrap, back out of her wigwam and tread home to my special place beneath the pin oak. I dig a deep hole, but before I bury it, I can't resist trying it on to see if it makes me feel any different.

Walks Like a Bear. Remove the headdress.

"Wolf? How did you know…I was just trying it…to see if I looked…do I have to give it back?" I whine.

Walks Like a Bear has not earned the honor to wear the eagle feather.

On the scale of embarrassments over my short life, this is on top. I refold the feather in the bark and cover my face with my paws.

I will tell you the tradition of the feather, says Wolf.

Stars fill a sky soaked with night. The trunks of trees snap and pop around me from the cold. *"Do I need to kill something before I wear this feather?"* I ask Wolf.

Eagle is the most war-like bird, Wolf says, *and the most highly respected of all birds. His feathers are unlike any others. This is the reason they are worn by The People to signify deeds of bravery. It is not true that when a brave wears a feather bonnet, each one of the feathers represents a coup. When a man wears one eagle feather upright on his head, it means he has performed four coups on his enemy.*

"Is a coup the killing of an enemy?"

No, it is the after-stroke or touching of the body after the enemy falls. This act is important because often the touching of an adver-

sary is much more difficult to accomplish than the shooting of one from a distance. It requires a strong heart to face the life you have taken. Many a brave has been lost in the attempt of counting his coup on the fallen, says the wolf.

When a warrior approaches his foe, dead or alive, he calls to the other warriors to witness by saying, 'This man performed the brave deed of counting a coup upon the body of the bravest of our enemies.' When the war party returns, the courageous deeds are announced publicly. Those who were present to witness the act, testify they saw it. Any brave who wears the eagle's feather must have given proof before his tribe of his right to do so. The feather becomes part of a warrior's record on his headdress.

I scratch my ear to help remember.

Wolf continues. *If a brave is wounded in the same battle where he performed his coup, he wears the feather hanging downward. When he is wounded, but has made no coup, he trims his feather and it does not need to be the feather of an eagle. All other feathers are merely ornaments.*

"Would it take long for a young brave to learn the feather rules, as long as it is taking me?" I say to Wolf.

Listen and remember this forever. When a warrior wears a feather with a round mark, it means he has slain his enemy. When the mark is red, it means he has taken the scalp. When a brave has slain as many enemies as you can count toenails on both your front paws, he is entitled to a war-bonnet.

"Wolf, if I kill a mole and then touch it can I wear a feather?"

No. Recognized leaders are permitted to wear war bonnets with long, trailing plumes. Those who count even more coups can tip the ends of the feathers with bits of fluffy white or colored down.

"How about a spider if I'm caught in its web? Would that count?"

No. Sometimes the eagle feather is tipped with a strip of weasel skin. This means the wearer has the honor of killing, scalping, and counting the first coup on the enemy all at the same time.

"If I don't kill or scalp anyone, will I ever be eligible to wear a feather?"

You can wear any other kind of feather, but not an eagle's, says Wolf. *Although, sometimes one is worn on great occasions by the child of a noted brave, to indicate the father's dignity and position.*

I sense Wolf is watching as I bury the birch bark package. I push two flat rocks on top to mark the spot. I haven't heard of a scalping or a coup of or by a dog since I came to live at Clark Lake. I did see a lady wearing a raccoon coat in Jackson. I wonder if she counted coup when she killed that creature.

I think of my father, Ken Bear's Pippin, and wonder if he ever attempted a courageous deed during his lifetime that would qualify me to wear an eagle feather. I remember the silver trophies that lined the halls at our kennel. Winning a trophy beats killing and scalping any day in my world. I've got to find another feather. Maybe the crows have left one… or the owl. Wolf is still watching me. I wonder if I could ever earn a trophy at a dog show.

My brain is addled. I try to remember all that I have agreed to do. Calle says sometime soon the most important event of my life will occur when I have the dream of my youth. She says it is the custom for a Potawatomi warrior to think about this dream and try to solve it for the rest of his life. A true warrior keeps the secret and only on his dying bed speaks of the dream.

The trees at the end of the lake are like a line of blue fog, a deep, feathery, gray-blue silhouette below the setting sun. It's time for me to lay with my muzzle facing into the wind. I fall asleep with a stiff breeze blowing over my big, black, capricious nose.

FORTY

I'm coming across our lawn just as Elizabeth and Officer Diesel come outside…almost stepping on Elizabeth's old backpacks.

"Herbie honey, you've found my backpacks. What's wrong? Why are you sad?"

"Is that the original backpack your dog was wearing the day of the ATM robbery?" Officer Diesel asks as he picks up the dirty canvas bag. "Or is that the bogus one we had Herbie wear when we were setting up the kidnapper?"

"Yes, that one is the real one I stuffed it with a book on dog training and another on child psychology," Elizabeth points. "They were the heaviest weights I could find. I'm attempting to strengthen Herbie's legs so he will get muscular enough be in a show dog."

Officer Diesel lifts the flap on the muddy backpack. A broad smile radiates from his lips followed by convulsive laughter.

"What's so funny out there?" Bob says, coming to the front door. "What kind of trouble is that mutt in now?"

"I'm laughing because the entire Jackson Police Department couldn't solve these crimes. You and your wife couldn't solve these crimes. But your sheepdog could and did. Look at this." Officer Diesel pours the contents of the backpack onto the ground. I watch as Mrs. Howard's soup bones drop to the patio. I hide my head under my paws. "Here's the stolen money and the stolen credit cards, and here are your weight training manuals."

Elizabeth picks up her books and holds them out to Officer Diesel.

"You won't need this one," Officer Diesel says and takes the book on dog training. "I'll need one for evidence, and if you don't mind I'll keep it to use in our K-9 unit. You've done a wonderful job training Herbie. I'd sure like a detective like him on my team." The officer collects the green papers and plastic cards and stuffs the plunder into the dirt smudged bag.

"Thanks. I guess our Herbie isn't entirely stupid," says Bob, "and he is a hero for protecting my Elizabeth." He puts his arm around his wife. "Because he's such a good dog, he can have any treat he wants...in moderation...next week."

Who could argue that? Bob can have all the accolades from Officer Diesel and Elizabeth if only I can have these bones.

"But get rid of those bones, Elizabeth. They stink. I don't want our hero here getting sick." He reaches down and pets my head. "I'll get the garbage can," Bob says.

You poisonous toad!

"Herbie, don't growl. That's not nice," Elizabeth says, and then holds out her hand to Officer Diesel. "Thanks for all your help. Our family can finally get back to living our boring, nondescript lives: summer days without break-ins, robberies, kidnappings, police visits during the day and night, or my all- time personal favorite terrifying experience… being drugged and buried alive.

"Good bye, Mrs. Hartman," Officer Diesel says. He slips the backpack in his trunk, nods to Bob, and backs up the driveway.

"There must have been twenty-five thousand dollars and thirty or forty stolen credit cards in that back pack," Bob says.

"And all these weeks that money was buried in our garden. Elizabeth, I'll help you plant tulips next year. I wonder what else that hound has buried."

That blustering braggart is a lump of foul deformity in a moldy, leach-infested dunghill that even vile, debased worms would not touch. Besides, he's a nonstop promise breaker and an endless liar…and that's his good side.

FORTY-ONE

Puddles of moving water form on the blue lake ice melting from the longer hours of daylight. Waves lap against the margins of our shore. Water swishes and splashes a steady rhythm, a beat that makes the lake come alive. Spring is sprouting yellow-green snowdrops and daffodils. This change in season comes just as I am losing hope of ever feeling the penetrating heat of a steady sun on my bones, the warm glow that strokes and soothes my spine. I'm not afraid of change anymore.

If the worst happens, I'm confident I can find a channel around it without using violence. Today is the first whiff of promise, a time for fresh starts, a morning muscle stretch that makes the long run possible.

I have so much to do now that it's spring: bones to bury under the bush Elizabeth calls the cinnamon tipped hemlock and between the dry hydrangea stalks left standing after the winter snows, new scents to follow that lay hidden beneath the frozen crust, progress of the tulip, daffodil and narcissus to monitor after the deer have fed on them, checking the lake for icebergs, ducks, and wolf pups.

During the last leg of my busy morning walk with Calle she warns me about a bald eagle that is nesting across the lake. "We are in his hunting territory."

I stopped walking. "What do eagles eat?"

"Small animals…rabbits, squirrels, moles, even raccoon. They eat ducks, all sorts of birds and snakes. They eat injured animals and the old and feeble."

"Dogs?" I back under a bush. I'm getting nervous.

Calle laughs. "Not big ones like you. You're too heavy for an eagle to lift."

"What about skinny dogs like you?" I find a big bush and wiggle under.

"You're right. I used to be a large dog. Now I'm just a bag of bones. I may have a few parts left that would taste sweet to a buzzard or an eagle."

"Do eagles circle in the sky above their prey?" I can see the eagle clearly through the bush and my knees are shaking.

"I've seen them circle a large fish in the lake, swoop down with their talons extended and grab the fish before it knows it's even a target for the big bird's lunch."

"Do eagles have a white head and brown wings?" The winged creature is beginning his dive.

"There are several kinds of eagles," Calle continues. "The ones that hunt our lake have a white underbelly. And yes, their heads are white. They have a yellow hooked nose."

"And yellow feet…big yellow…" I can see the scales and the needle-like curved talons.

"Walks Like a Bear, how do you know so much about eagles?"

"An eagle is circling overhead right now."

"What?" Red Dog crouches to the ground and looks up. "I can't see that far. Where is the bird?"

"He's right there. His wing span is enormous."

"Are his circles getting smaller?" I back further into the bush and as close to the fence as I can.

"I can see his beak. It's yellow like his feet."

"Herbie, stop with the descriptions already. How near us is he?"

"Duck!"

"Hide next to the fence, Herbie. Quick. I'll join you. Where is the fence?"

"Over here. I'm already hiding, Calle." I see the eagle swoop, extend his yellow talons and snag Calle.

"Ahiiii! He's got me! Help!"

"I thought you were too big for the eagle."

"Sometimes I'm wrong. Ouch! Help me Herbie."

I can see the large bird struggle to get Calle off the ground. Red Dog is reaching her head around attempting to bite the eagle's leg, putting up a good fight. "Calle, I'm scared." I cover my eyes with my paws.

"You're scared? I'm the one he's marked for lunch!"

"What should I do?" I peek out and see some feathers float in the air. She's putting up an amazing fight for such an old dog.

"Think! Then act. I don't have much time. His talons are digging deeper. He's hurting me."

"I'll get Elizabeth."

"There's no time. Help me! Use what you learned from the legends."

"Which legend? Which one?" My knees shake until they give out and I drop to the ground. From where I am hiding I see Eagle extend his talons. From where I am leaning against the fence I see the powerful bird insert his claws into the base of what's left of my friend's tail. From where I stand trembling I watch the hunter hook his yellow beak into the scruff of my mentor's neck. This flying menace releases his talons and my best friend's rear legs fall toward the ground. The birds wings are spread so wide I can barely see Eagle whip the Irish setter from side to side. I hear a snap. Calle O'Riley hangs limp from its beak like a wet rag on a hook.

Not one creature comes to her aid. No birds chirp for Eagle to stop hurting the former Keeper of the Potawatomi Legends. No crows caw to insist Eagle drop Calle, their friend who brokered the truce between us. No rabbits thump a threat in her defense. Squirrels hide. Even the black walnuts cease dropping from the tree by the lake.

I feel no wind. The lake is silent. The air is so quiet I can hear a leaf drop and skid across the lawn. It's like our whole world is holding its breath. I bark with hope in my heart, "Calle? Are you sleeping old girl? Is this another of your lessons for me?"

No answer, but Eagle is standing so close to me that when he turns his head, he looks into my eyes. Red Dog is dangling from his beak. I understand his message, crouch with fear and back deeper into the fence. The giant bird that rules from the sky stands tall, flaps his wings, and carries the carcass of Calle O'Riley into the sky.

My old friend floats beneath and behind her nemesis as they soar up and over Clark Lake, glaze the tree tops of Eagle Point and disappear into the distant sky. Red Dog is flying into the afterworld with an eagle.

And I'm the coward who let her die.

FORTY-TWO

It has been several suns since Calle soared with Eagle. I'm still hoping she will fly back to Clark Lake and return to her home next door, but it could be I will never see her again. On my morning walk with Elizabeth, Mrs. O'Riley emerges from her cottage and waves us to stop. She is pale. I smell sadness.

"Calle disappeared on Thursday afternoon," she says to Elizabeth. "I made lost dog reward posters for around the lake. She may have been stolen. She was old and had trouble moving. She may have been hit by a fast moving car. I drove the lake roads and checked for her body on paths skirting the ditch. She may have slipped, fallen into the open water and drowned. I asked but no ice fishermen have seen her floating under the ice. I did find two sets of tracks on the ice. She may have been chasing a coyote." Mrs. O'Riley starts to cry. "My intuition tells me my sweet Irish setter is gone forever."

I lower my head. My happiness melts away like the winter ice. I'm responsible for Mrs. O'Riley's tears. She will hate me when she learns I let her dog fly with Eagle. It's suddenly hard to breathe. My best friend was in trouble and I was too frightened to help her. My knees collapse. I feel like vomiting. Elizabeth will be ashamed of my cowardice. I let everyone down. I'm no good.

I slide into a puddle of slush. My nose sinks into the cold snow. Twin drips trickle toward the tip. They are not raindrops, although the afternoon has become cloudy and sad enough.

"I am so sorry," I hear Elizabeth say. "We will miss her, especially Herbie. They spent so much time together." I see her give Mrs. O'Riley a hug and pat her back. "I hope you find her and I sure hope she's all right."

I wish I could hear Mrs. O'Riley say, "We found her and buried her under the hedge-row juniper in the woodlot behind the cottage." I recall Calle telling me I would know where a dog with soongetcha would be buried when it was their time, but now I'll never know. Eagle didn't honor the Potawatomi tradition for this Keeper of the Legends. It's my fault she isn't buried with her equals.

Elizabeth's eyes tear. She watches Mrs. O'Riley walk across her empty yard, step inside the old white cottage and quietly close the door.

Layers of wailings rise and fall from inside my chest. I am ashamed. I weep for Calle. Or is crying something cowards do to feel better? Calle fought Eagle. Why didn't I bark or bite or bang against Eagle? Could I have pulled her away from the grip of those talons? Could I have stopped Eagle from breaking her old neck? Why did I let myself be paralyzed by fear?

I can't stay here. I don't deserve to walk where she walked. I don't want Elizabeth to see me like this, and I can't stand my own company. I need to chuck out my grief somewhere else.

I hold the howl inside my cheek until I have passed the O'Riley woodlot. My feet fly over a field, charge along a ridge until I find myself deep in the forest. I'm bone tired. I drop on a bed of dry needles beneath a balsam tree. The ache growing deep inside my bowels pushes up my throat, develops into a wail and bursts from my muzzle in a loud, convulsing sob. I lay on my side, my grief too heavy for my legs to bear. I hear myself howl until the hurt feels neutralized and my tears are dry. I fall silent, lay still, breathing in shallow puffs.

In the filtered forest light I see a paw of seksi strolling in a grove of willows gazing at a fawn on the soft straw, newly born. The fawn is being cleaned by her mother's tongue and nudged by her nose to stand. The deer suspend their motion. Perhaps they caught my scent. A buck with a long facial scar braves the point to protect his family. He signals danger with a steady front leg stomp, then waits and watches. I don't move. The stag ambles towards me, stops and looks down at my aching heart.

"Do not cry Walks Like a Bear." The buck stretches his neck and lowers his head so we can speak privately. "We all grow up and like trees return to nature to make way for saplings," he whispers to me. "Buried in the woodland besides Barks at Birds are Yellowed-Fox, Fish-Lure-Stained-Blue, Line-of-Thunder, White Otter Dog, Strong-Ground, Hole-in-the-Day, and Blue. They all carried the legends. Eagle knows we are all part of nature's path. He will do what is right."

"How do you know all this?"

"Most animals have heard the legends. You are different, Walks Like a Bear. You must remember all of the legends. You are the Nidjikiwese, the Keeper…" The buck's body bolts abruptly to attention. I see his muscles tighten under burnished brown skin. His long ears turn independently on each side of his skull, listening, alerted to danger by the snap of a twig.

I crank my neck and catch the familiar scent.

The stag flags danger to his family with his tail straight up. Before the doe understands the threat, I spring to my feet and place myself between the wolf and the new mother. She is still nudging her fawn to stand. A warning growl erupts from my throat as molten courage pours inside my veins. I step toward the beast and block his view of the fawn. She is whimpering and wobbling toward her mother.

The wolf steps forward.

Instinctively my lips draw back as a ferocious growl screams from my throat. My teeth are bared. I push forward, the hunted threatening the hunter. I cross to the downed tree separating us and jump over the log, snapping my fangs as I growl.

The gray wolf steps back, turns and lopes toward the field of maize stubble. His gait has a hint of a limp. We all watch as he disappears into the forest beyond.

Spitting the growl from my mouth I take a deep breath and turn to survey the scene. No one is moving. The deer stare at me. My knees shake. The quaking moves up my hind limbs and along my spine. "What just happened?" I say aloud.

"It was your instinct, a power from deep inside, Walks Like a Bear. It was your soongetcha," whispers the stag.

"I am grateful to you for your strong heart," the doe says softly, side-stepping to redirect her wandering fawn back into the herd.

"This is Red Dog's choice for Nidjikiwesi, and our friend who has promised to carry the legends," the old buck barks for the forest to hear. "Thank you for saving my new daughter." He bays and motions toward the fawn, now walking on her own. And with that, the big buck turns and disappears deep into the cedar swamp followed closely by his family. Perhaps they are searching for a safe winter home, a yard where hundreds of deer will be protected from the weather.

Tracing my scent back from the forest to the O'Riley woodlot, I imagine my mentor flying the length of the Milky Way. Yes, Barks at Birds will be the dog standing watch on the path of the dead, the Tibekana, making sure Red Dog does not return.

FORTY-THREE

"Herbie, you will turn into a mushroom if you stay inside the cottage where it's so stuffy," Elizabeth says. She opens the door and waits. "Maybe we should see Dr. Hauschild."

"No," I whine, get to my feet and lumber over the threshold and into the crisp evening air. My pace is swifter while she's watching, my trot bolder. I examine every scent and sound in the yard, watch every blade of grass as it twists and leaf as it flutters until she closes the door. Then my shoulders slump, my step slows and my vigor stalls. My feet flop and my belly droops. I stroll to the shore and give in to the ground.

Round stones by the seawall stand heather-speckled. They look like a German shepherd's winter fur and remind me that Beau Schmidt is now my only friend. I study burnished auburn stones, rough and jagged, like Red Dog's patchy coat. The Irish setter had been my first friend, my mentor. I could have saved her. My life is now marked by guilt.

A stick snaps from somewhere behind me. I jump, spin my head, glance left then right. No threat. I stand on the dusky seawall and return to pawing black and shaggy white rocks, the ones that look like my own hair, tangled in bad behavior. I inspect one stone and push it away. I lay down on the ground to reflect, my rumpled head spreading wide and flat on the sandstone.

My imagination ascends to the Milky Way. "Hello Red Dog. I'm sorry, old friend. Are you disappointed in me?" I growl softly. My old teacher's red face appears, blurs, and then turns into an amber cornerstone. "Can you feel it when I think of you?"

The kitchen door opens. I hear Bob raging, dazzling the world with his anger. "Look at this. Look what I found right in the center of the sidewalk." He is holding something brown and hard in his hand. "You've got to do something about this, Elizabeth."

"What is it?" she asks the man who smells like stupid.

"It looks like dog scat."

"These are dog turds. Two of them,"

"Why are you holding dog feces?"

"I want you to see what I almost stepped in."

"Bob?" Elizabeth sticks her head outside and scans the yard.

"Close the door. You're letting all the heat out."

"I'm checking on Herbie. He's depressed. The dog next door disappeared last Thursday. She was Herbie's best friend."

"Give me a break. Dogs don't get depressed. Dogs don't have feelings," Bob says. "Dogs don't have best friends." Elizabeth closes the door and I can hear her scolding him.

As the night thickens, sifting sounds like sand sliding down a dune hiss a counterpoint to the rhythm of lapping waves. I can see in the dark as well as the day, yet I didn't notice the twinkling yellow eyes watching me from above, waiting.

Lacking focus, my vision wanders back to smaller stones. I look for the finest, smoothest stones. I find a brown stone that looks honed to form a point. The sight spurs Red Dog's stories hibernating inside my mind. I recall her telling how Potawatomi braves sat for hours chipping flint and obsidian stones. Deer antlers were used to chip tips for spears, hatchets and hunting arrows.

Budding memories leaf out into the open air. I recall her telling about the order of food eaten at a feast around campfire stones, a meal prepared by women to celebrate a hunter's success or to welcome a stranger. When food was plentiful, she told me the meal had four courses.

The first platter was usually white fish simmered in a water-filled clay pot heated by dropping in red-hot stones. The second stone platter left at the fires edge held boiled tongue and breast meat from a deer. The third stone platter held two wood hens, the hind feet of a bear, and the tail of a beaver. And the fourth course was a large quantity of broth made from several kinds of meats. Soup was spiced with herbs prepared on a grinding stone. Maple syrup was mixed with water to make a sweet drink served with the meal. As Red Dog told me about the feast, I grew hungry. I have not been hungry like that since my old friend passed.

I look up to see a familiar star blinking stronger than before. I wonder if…but before I finish wondering, I hear a fallen leaf at the gatepost of my yard bruised and crushed by a large paw. I don't respond because I'm rubbing away a heavy tear sliding down my cheek that I want to hide. The endless suns I spent with Red Dog learning Potawatomi legends are mine to nurture into flowers and then pass on as essence.

Snap! Behind me a shattering sound cuts the air. Before me lake ice clatters like breaking windowpanes. Beside me snow-crust crunches. It is the moon when frost sparkles and magnifies emotions. I see the silhouette of Beau Schmidt, the regal German shepherd who has been waiting at my side-yard door.

Fear has overtaken my grief since Red Dog soared into the sky. Fear has overtaken my ability to eat or sleep, or to leave my yard alone. I mark the border of my property with a stronger scent message. No one is allowed to enter without permission except for my family and special friends. I tip my head to Beau, an invitation to come forward.

A rancid scent fills Beau's nose. He shakes his head and sneezes to send the scent away. Regaining his noble composure, he joins me at the seawall.

"My heart is on the ground. I grieve for Red Dog, too," Beau says and settles beside me on the snow. The German shepherd is quiet for some time, then whispers, "Suffering is only letting go of things that don't vork anymore." He stares over the lake as he speaks. "The old dog lived vith pain each day. It vas time for her to go."

"No Beau. I let the eagle take her."

Beau whisked a dried leaf off his shoulder with his nose. "You suffer because it's time for you to grow. On the other side of suffering is belief." He turns his head. "Calle believed in you. Now you must believe in you. It's okay to cry, even for one who valks like a bear."

"I am not crying." I lie. "It's those bright stars poking holes in the sky. They sting my eyes."

"Of course they do." Beau speaks softly. "But all your tears vill vash avay the day and the next day and the next unless you allow me to help. Let's take all these seavall stones, throw them into the sky and block the holes behind the stars. Vould you feel better then?"

"No."

Beau sees my frown furrow, my lips quiver, and my tears flow.

"You don't know what I didn't do," I tell him. "If you knew that I didn't help her fight the Eagle…"

"You saw the great bird take Red Dog avay? Valks Like a Bear, vhen you see Eagle you are put on notice to stretch your limits, push yourself to be more than you think you are. Eagle expects you to look ahead. But vhen Eagle attacks like he did with Red Dog it means she had some problems she needed to push past. She went soaring with Eagle to expand her view.

"Red Dog trusted you to keep the Potavatomi history. She chose you to be Nidjikivesi, Keeper of the Legend. She vill be vatching to make sure you do. Think of it this vay. Vhen puppies are born they have large feet. As they grow their bodies and hearts expand to fit their big feet. Now you must grow to fill the paw prints of the Nidjikiwesi. Vas that all vhat vas bothering you?"

"I don't want to be the Nidjikiwesi anymore. I don't deserve it. I hate it. I hate this stone. I hate this tree. I hate being afraid. I hate myself for not helping my best friend when she begged me for help."

"Herbie, speak to the tree. Apologize," says Beau. He watches as I get up, walk over and sink my teeth into the tree.

"I didn't say attack the tree. I said speak to the tree. You must listen more closely."

I fidget, slump in the snow, my head drooping until my nose touches the ground.

Beau's voice grows firm. "Now look into the sky and apologize to Red Dog. You are the Nidjikivesi. I expect more from you. I expect more."

I shake my head to stop my nose from flowing. I blurt out between sobs, "She was not buried according to the custom."

"So that is it... Calle O'Riley's bones vere not buried next to the other Nidjikivesi? Don't you know she vas honored to be picked by an eagle? Didn't she tell you how grateful she vould be if she could soar with the largest and bravest bird in our vorld? Every dog dreams of being carried so high they can be forever behind the night sky blinking at dogs like you and me? Red Dog is now a star in the Milky Way? Isn't that enough?"

"No," I say. "The body should have been placed on a scaffold for three suns. Her friends would have conducted a special ceremony to celebrate the departure of the soul from Red Dog's body. She told me that is the way of the People. That should also be the way of the Peoples' dogs."

"Herbie, solve a mystery for me." Beau said. "Did you pee on the gate tree or vas it the two-legged alpha male that lives vith you? Those marks on your boundary trees are putrid. They assault my nostrils."

"Extra security."

"Then it vas your vork. How did you get that particular odor…eat the scent from a stink root veed?" Beau shakes his snout and sneezes again.

I exhale and stare straight ahead. I sniff, still brooding over my loss.

"Come vith me, Herbie. I vant to show you something…a secret Potawatomi burial mound. You must promise never to show it to people."

"Why would a burial place be secret?" I ask. "Calle told me Native Americans consider a cemetery to be a sacred place, for visiting or for sad occasions. When someone in a band dies it is the custom for close relatives to wash the body and dress it in the best clothing…if it's a person. If it's an animal they roll it in the best blanket and place it in a low peaked wooden structure, a spirit house, with the feet pointed to the west, the direction of the spirit's journey. Calle told me markers were placed at the grave to indicate the totem, the family's history. For a few sleeps after the burial, fires are kept burning nearby and food is placed on a ledge at a small hole in the western end of the spirit house where the spirit will emerge from the body.

"Nowadays some people poke their shovels in holy places," Beau says, "digging in graves…looking for old pottery, jewelry, arrowheads. They collect sacred objects, put them in boxes in closets and forget about them. It's better if they don't know this location," Beau says and trots from my yard.

I follow him to the north wind road where we are careful not to cross until we can no longer hear the putter of cars. We angle down a steep ditch and around a fallen tree trunk.

"This vay, Herbie," Beau says, boiling dust in his wake. "Behind this field is a cedar svamp vhere the vhite tailed deer yard up in vinter. Then just beyond that is a small pond circled by trees, the sacred burial grounds."

"Okay, Beau, but don't go so fast. My chest aches for air."

"That's not from running your feet, my friend," Beau says, turning his head so I can see the big smile on his face.

It is so good to have a friend like Beau as I cross this second growth forest. His teasing keeps me grounded. I duck under the drooping yellow hawkweed. I know I talk too much, and he's right about my moping about Calle. I need to stop, but it's so hard because she was such an exceptional animal. I jump over an abandoned wheelbarrow. I want him to know everything about her. A doe lifts her head from a stream as we pass. I want everyone to know. I'm enjoying this adventure with Beau even though we cross over wild grape vines with thorns that snare my coat. The old hedge rider stops when I bark, comes back and pulls the vines free that are caught in the long hair of my legs. Something exciting always happens when I'm with Beau Schmidt.

Beau stops moving, inhales the cold air and reads the wind. "Looks like a storm is brewing. See those dark clouds?" he says as we enter the swamp where the lichens crust the rocks red. My friend chooses a path without briars in my honor. I see dark clouds moving across the sky.

I jump over fallen trees, scramble under a rusty fence and follow the worn path of a wabasog. I smell pine needles and damp, rich earth. The trees are so close they form a barricade keeping the blue sky from being seen on the forest floor.

"Crack!" I hear a sound like a watermelon splitting open after it drops on the floor. "Crack!" I hear brush moving…like a large animal is turning inside a dense thicket. "Crack!" The noise is coming from the forest canopy. I look up and jump back just as a limb crashes down.

I spit unnatural words as it shoves me into the ooze of last season's leaves, stagnant water and green slime. "Beau? Wolf? Elizabeth?" The sudden pressure on my chest knocks out my memories. Pain stabs my shoulder. My foreleg feels useless. I'm under water.

My first days at Clark Lake soak my memories. I remember the time the lake tried to swallow me. I vowed then this would not happen again. I kick my hind legs until I locate a submerged limb and push until my snout emerges from the slime. I can breathe. I cough. My paw instinctively pushes off another limb that's holding me. I struggle forward and upward until I can stand.

"Beau?" I bark. "Where are you?"

"I'm here. Ahhh," he exhales what sounds like pain, "trapped."

"Can you move at all?" I hop on three legs along the high ground toward the sound of his voice. My front shoulder aches. "I can't see you. Bark something."

A dull whisper of a growl comes from the murky water beside me. I turn to see his elegant head in the mud, and his body pinned by the crotch of a fallen tree. The rain is crashing down in torrents making its way through the filigree of limbs above. It's a deluge. The water is cold. It's hard to see.

"Beau, don't move. I'll dig you out."

"Hurry, the vater is rising."

"A good time to keep your mouth shut is when the water is rising," I say and hobble down into the muck. I can see part of his gray-black leg and one black boot. "I'll get you out."

Calle told me if I get in trouble and fall under the ice, I should hold on and call for help. We're so far out in the woods no person would hear me. I scratch away muck with my front paw and try anyway. Bark-bark-bark! I wait, and then repeat the distress signal used by all native tribes. Bark-bark-bark! Calle told me the People used puffs of smoke from a campfire, shots from a gun or beats on a drum. They all work if the pattern is repeated three times. Bark-bark-bark. Dig-dig-dig.

"Herbie?"

"Yes Beau."

"There's a stick poking me. It hurts."

"Where?" I hobble around to his head.

"My chest." He's gasping. His eyes are closed. He's squinting from pain.

I lower my head underwater, follow his neck down to where I feel a twig has punctured the skin on his brisket. I pull the pointed branch with my teeth, jerking it backwards until it slips out. I return to the surface with the prize in my mouth to the sound of Beau's painful howl.

"Thank you for stopping the poker from burning me, but my back…I'm pinched, and the vater is getting higher. I don't think I'm going to make it."

"Bark-bark-bark! Dig-dig-dig! Bark-bark-bark!" I howl until my lungs feel like they're bleeding. Calle told me never to give up. Never. There is always a way. There is a channel. I keep digging.

I look up to see a white tail stag watching. I can see a familiar scar on the side of his face. He nudges the limb with his hoof. It won't budge. I join him by throwing my weight against the large branch. It moves far enough for him to push another limb under it.

Dig-dig-dig. Dig-dig-dig.

"Herbie?"

"Yes Beau?"

The shepherd stretches his chin up like he's making a pronouncement. "You've been a good friend, Herbie. Keep your soongetcha." That's all he says. The rising water comes into his white ears.

"No!" I bark. "Don't give up," I howl, scrambling my back paws into action. Wet leaves and swamp slime fly in a solid stream behind me. I reach under the water with my muzzle, grasp the scruff of Beau's neck and pull. I can feel him move and then stop. I come up for air, and return for another pull. This time when I surface Beau's head comes with me above the water line. He gasps for air and coughs. Blood drizzles down his cheek.

Raindrops pierce the swamp water aching to be Beau's grave, their circles widening, reaching out to his chest. The buck is pushing the limb again, taking the pressure off Beau as I pull the shepherd farther up the bank toward the high ground. Beau is able to push with his back feet to help until none of us can push any longer.

"Never give up, Beau. Let's try again." I look up at the stag. "Never-never-never!" The stag is pushing the limb again with his rack. I pull the hide along Beau's neck. He kicks his way free. I'm ready to collapse on the high ground, exhausted, but I feel something biting my ear.

I look up to see the stag. When I try to stand the pain in my shoulder returns. Sunrays sliding from the forest canopy dim. I grow dizzy yet my rear legs push me upright. The stag continues to nudge me with his soft nose until I find myself on high ground.

"Walks Like a Bear," barks the stag. "Can you and the German shepherd walk? It's a long way to your homes. Would you like a drink before we start?"

"We need a drink of water like we need a plague of hydrophobia. Let's go Beau. I've still got three good legs. We had better get out of here while we can."

"The water rises fast in this swamp," says the stag. "Follow me. I will guide you to safety."

Beau nods and stumbles up the embankment. Wobbling on three legs, I follow the stag along a well-worn ridge bordered with briars, prickly wild grape vines, and a thicket of scrub trees. We cross under older trees and into the field before the stag recommends I rest. "I'll walk back and help the German shepherd catch up," the stag says. When he returns he stands guard over us until we are ready to make our way across the open field. It's still raining hard.

When we get to the ditch before the north wind road, the white tail deer gets behind me and pushes my rump with the flat of his head. He shoves me up the hill to the side of the road. It's tough going. I can hear his grunting over my groaning from pain. Then he repeats the push for Beau who has fallen behind again.

The stag hears the car first. "Danger-danger-danger!" he barks, sets Beau down and lopes into a thicket at the side of the field. The car comes to a stop after it has already passed by. Bob steps out and walks toward me.

"Herbie, is that you?" he says looking down at my muck-soaked mass of twig and burr-entwined hair. "I've been driving around looking for you for an hour." Then he notices the blood on my shoulder. "Come, Herbie," he says calmly. Then in a lower, gentler tone he says, "Can you get into the back seat of my car? You need some help with that shoulder, boy. Let's go find Elizabeth." As Beau steps out on the road Bob says, "Is that the Schmidts' dog?"

Beau is wet. He rocks where he stands like he will fall at any time. His knees are wobbling.

"Herbie, you're bleeding," he says to me. "Come on big fella." He gets my strong front shoulder up on the back seat. "We can make it, Herbie. There you go. Lean that wounded shoulder on mine. We'll make it together. Up you go." He gives my rump a big shove and the mass of my mud is planted on his spotless leather upholstery.

I hear the distant roar of a car before I see the lights reflecting on the slick pavement. Through the back window I watch the alpha male of my pack take a few quick steps toward the wet and bleeding shepherd now sitting in the road shined with rain. It happens fast. I only get one warning out. "Bark-bark-bark!"

Beau understands. He pushes his exhausted body up, taking a step towards the shoulder when the bright eyes of the car appear. They're large and round like a night owl. The air fills with squeals and the smell of rubber skidding on pavement. Then I hear the thud.

Beau doesn't make a sound as he flies through the air. His path is illuminated by the vehicle's bright head lights. His body is all legs and tail and head as it curls in front of the sky, flying like Eagle. But, his path isn't to the Milky Way where Calle is watching and waiting for him. Instead he lands with an even louder thud on the roadside near where Bob is standing. The owl eyes on the vehicle now light an open field opposite the field of corn stubble, the same field the white tail pushed and pulled Beau and I across. The growl from the motor stops.

"What the hell are you doing parked on a curve?" a man screams at Bob who is kneeling, comforting the German shepherd.

"It's going to be all right, boy. I'll get you some help," Bob says to Beau.

"A dog? It's a dirty dog? A mangy animal wrecked my van?" the man says as he staggers towards Bob. "You'll pay to fix my car," he says. "I thought I hit a deer. Your stupid dog totaled the front end of my new van. I should finish him off." The man draws back one foot to kick Beau's broken body into the ditch.

I've never seen Bob move this fast. He is like a fox chasing a chicken. He grabs the man's shoulder with one hand, spins him around and smacks his fist into his jaw. The guy staggers backwards and falls on the pavement. Bob hovers over him.

"This dog is someone's pet. He has a life and a right to live just like you and me. Show some respect. Get up! Help me lift him into my trunk or you will experience the pain of flying though the air like this shepherd just did."

"Okay. Easy, mister. Slow down. No need to get physical. I'll help you."

"Open my trunk," Bob orders. "You take his head, hold it flat, brace his neck…he may have a spinal injury." They scoop Beau up in their arms, his broken and twisted legs hanging in odd angles from his torso.

I can't see anymore. My mind is shaken. Confusion doesn't sum it up. The trunk lid blocks my view. I can hear Beau moan as he settles on the soft carpet of the trunk floor. I can hear the trunk lid click shut. I see Bob jump behind the driving wheel.

"Lay down, Herbie," Bob says to me. The motor growls and the car lunges forward. The man appears smaller out the back window as he staggers after us shaking his fist. I lie down as instructed and hear Bob talking into his hand. "Elizabeth, call the vet. Tell him I'm on my way with two emergencies. Yes, he's alive. The other dog is that friend of his, that German shepherd…yes, you better call the Schmidts'. He's banged up bad. Yes, I'll drive carefully. See you there. I love you, too."

The car fills with the too-sweet stench of fresh blood. Hearing Bob in this gentle, helpful state almost neutralizes the pain in my shoulder. Somehow I suspected this alpha male would be ready to help when his pack needed him.

Dr. Hauschild chases Beau's pain away first with a shot while the shepherd is still bleeding in Bob's trunk. I see them carry Beau in on a board then return for me.

I can hear Dr. Schmidt soothing Beau in the next room. Mrs. Schmidt is weeping.

When the doctor finishes with Beau, he comes into the room where Bob has carried me and lain me on this white tablecloth. He doesn't seem to notice the mud on my coat. He's more interested in moving my front leg around. He gives me a shot in the neck to help the pain run away while Elizabeth holds my head. "Be careful," he advises her. "He's hurting and may try to nip you, again." He gives Elizabeth pills for my discomfort and sends us home, me with a sling on my leg and a band snapped around my brisket.

The pills put me to sleep. My dreams are of Calle in the sky, watching from the Milky Way. "Never, never, never give up," she is barking to the stars or anyone who will listen.

FORTY-FOUR

I don't remember how I got into Elizabeth's station wagon or much of the ride to the hospital. I am still groggy as we wait to see the doctor. The floor is cool on my belly, pleasant. It hurts when I get on a gurney that smells of new paint. The entire place is too clean, has the appalling scent of disinfectant. This isn't Doctor Hauschild's clinic. I catch the scent of animals I don't recognize. I hear a cat howl.

I barely recall the roar of clippers and the scissor attack. I do remember being drenched with water, smeared with soap, rinsed with something hot. My senses remain dulled. It becomes quiet.

I wake in this cheerless crate. My shoulder hurts. My foot stings. My nose throbs. My right ear itches. I can't move my foot to scratch because I'm all taped together. My teeth prickle. My butt smarts. Something's biting my shoulder, a heat-stake, like stepping on hot pavement. The pain stabs up my neck and makes me weary.

"Aooow!" I vomit. "Where am I" Elizabeth? I want to see Bob. My mind must be sick. Did I just say I wanted to see Bob? I did, and I do. Then I remember the storm and Beau. "Aooow!" Howling helps scare the pain away. "Can someone help me? Is anyone out there?"

A mangy hound with outsized teeth throws his weight against my pen so violently in his enthusiasm to get at me that my pain is temporarily replaced with fear. My imagination roams to the Milky Way. "Calle, can you see me? Can you feel my pain?" At last I sleep.

"Mrs. Hartman, your dog is just down this aisle." I see the thin man in the white coat say as he comes around the corner by my pen. I've heard the other white coats call the string bean 'Matt.'

"I can find Herbie myself by following his howl," says a voice familiar to me.

Elizabeth? I thought she had abandoned me, given me away for medical research, or sent me to be euthanized. My voice is hoarse from howling from the pain. My world is a terrible place.

"Hello sweetheart," a voice familiar to me says.

Sweetheart? I hurt all over. Try 'Hello swollen heart,' or 'Hello bruised and battered heart.'

"How are you feeling?"

I am not comforted by Elizabeth's voice. How would she feel if she'd been tortured? I've never felt worse.

"Why are you crying?" She sticks her hand inside the bars of the pen to pet me.

"I wouldn't do that," the string bean warns, and pulls her arm back. "He almost took my hand off during the night." He removes a bandage to show Elizabeth.

"I'm sorry," she says and looks at the two small stitches holding the slit together on his palm. "What did you give my dog to kill the pain after you set his shoulder?"

"Mrs. Hartman, we tried, but he wouldn't let us near him. He snarled and tried to bite the doctor, too."

"Aren't you a doctor?"

"Not yet. I'm a vet student. I have two years to go."

"Do you mean to say this sheepdog has been suffering since the operation two days ago without anything to numb his pain? No wonder he bit you, Matt. I FEEL LIKE BITING YOU MYSELF!" she shouts. Lowering her voice, she orders, "Get me a dose of a strong pain killer. Do it now! I'll administer it myself."

Matt cowers. "Yes ma'am." He returns with a syringe. "Mrs. Hartman, first clean the area with this cotton soaked in alcohol to prevent infection. Then pinch the muscle on his neck between your index finger and your thumb. Insert the hypodermic needle with your other hand. Push the plunger down slowly…count to seven. Then withdraw it. Got it?"

"Yes, I've got it. Will you please open the cage?"

"Sure, but you're on your own in there. Hold it. There you go." The string bean hides behind the out-swung door as Elizabeth moves inside.

Am I glad to see a familiar face, even if it is one that left me here to die. I lick her hand while she pricks my shoulder. "Where have you been? I needed you." I whimper into her hair and wipe my tears on her blouse.

"It's okay, Herbie. I'm here to take you home. Just as soon as you get sleepy we'll load you in the station wagon. You can nap in the car. We'll take the highway…mmm…cottage. Wake up Herbie. We're home. Wake up, sweetheart." She rubs my head carefully so she doesn't touch the white bandage on my shoulder.

"Come inside, Herbie," drifts a voice that sounds like Bob. I cock my ear to hear. He actually sounds glad to see me. "He's still groggy," I hear him say. "I'll take his head and shoulders. Elizabeth, you grab his hips. Easy does it. Let's take him inside by the fireplace. Can you hold the door? Good. Yes I can close it. Be gentle, Elizabeth. Herbie's ordeal has been a nightmare."

"…Herbie, wake up. Drink some water sweetheart," she says. "You don't want to dehydrate. Then we'll go outside…"

"Emm…what is a dehydrate?" I say and try to turn over. Pain stabs my shoulder. I whine and turn back.

"Time for another shot, Bob. Will you give it to him this time?"

When I crack my eyes to test the forehead of the new day, I'm already outside. I see a dusky gray and white landscape. A blink later, a spit of red appears dusting the tips of the trees at the foot of the snow covered lake.

"I need your help today, great sun," I say, then settle into the soft snow waiting to let the Great Spirit's dose of heat and inspiration enter my body and settle into my shoulder. The crimson halo in the sky widens. Within two breaths I can see a clear red curve moving upwards. I open my mouth to the sun's rays and drink down the heat that soaks into my coat. I hold the extra warmth for later. "Will you be there today for the pain when I move my shoulder?"

As I wait for an answer from the Great Spirit, a blue cloud sneaks out of the darkness and completely covers the sun. "Coward!" I swear. "On all other sleeps when the world is my personal pot roast, you bellow the news with your light. On all other sleeps when I'm surrounded by shin-bone eating friends and a two-moon happiness reserve you warm the marrow in my stolen bones to make them taste better. Why is this day different than all others? Because," I bark to answer the spineless sun myself, "because I'm afraid and I'm losing hope that the pain won't go away and I want to see if my friend Beau Schmidt is okay." I begin to whimper. "And, because I'm really afraid he will die."

Just then a flare of light springs straight up from the cloud, an arrow in the sky, dominant like a confident dog's tail. The heat from the solar mass gradually burns a hole in the black cloud, a deep purple, then a red-violet, then a blast of crimson flame.

Walks Like a Bear, speak with respect when you address the Great Spirit. Remember who you are. You will have help. I have always come before, and I will always come again. Beau is alive and will recover.

Awestruck by the dazzle, I freeze, roll to my side, and expose my soft underside signing complete submission to the sun. "Let's not argue, wolf. I accept that you're in charge around here." The single ray seems to open, expand, filling the gray sky with warm purple, then gray-blue. I lie there on my back, my legs in the air, allowing hope to sink into my belly.

The kitchen door opens, and Elizabeth announces, "It's time for your shot, Herbie. Are you ready?"

I don't remember much from those first sleeps, and I never find out what a 'dehydrate' is. When I do feel better I drink a bowl of water. Bob carries me outside to pee when he gets home from work.

"Elizabeth, he urinates for a full two minutes. I never dreamed he could have a bladder that large."

"He has twelve-hour kidneys. You know he can hold it that long. Remember the time we were caught in traffic, and… buildup, and… control tower… Reed Road? Did I tell you the Schmidts' dog is home from the hospital? He has a punctured lung, and a broken hip and back leg. It was touch and go for a time, but he's going to be fine. Did you know he has had epileptic seizures since he was a pup? Elizabeth removes the bandage from my shoulder, revealing a hairless leg.

I gasp. This isn't my leg. It's the bony leg of a greyhound. Where is my leg? I wiggle my foot. It feels like mine. My leg shrunk. Hasn't anyone been feeding me? What happened to the long hair that covered this skinny leg? I am shocked.

"Who was the sneak that shaved my leg while I was sleeping?" I bark and look around for wolf tracks.

"Calm down, Herbie. I'm not going to hurt you," Elizabeth says as she applies sticky gunk to my leg that smells way too clean. "You've been dreaming." She wraps me again in white bandages. I get another shot and grow sleepy…and have more bad dreams…and get more shots.

"The Schmidts' dog, that German shepherd, looks like he could be a fighter. I wonder how the two of them got so beat up," Bob says. "The vet said it didn't look like they were in a dog fight."

"Herbie."

"Grrr."

"Herbie, don't turn your head away when I talk to you. Wake up."

"Wooof," I say, lifting my head from my crossed paws, and turning towards her. "Why can't you leave me alone?" I let my chin drop like a sack of sand. "Can't a dog have some peace and quiet around here?"

"Herbie, your leg is healed and you haven't moved all day."

"Is there a creature in this world sensitive enough to understand how much I still hurt? My shoulder itches, my neck smarts, and my leg lost all its hair," I whine.

"Come on sweetheart," Elizabeth says. "You need some exercise."

I get up slowly, one leg at a time, follow her with my head down, trip and almost fall forward when my front paw pins my beard. "Ouch!" I start to cry.

"You silly goose," she says, walking back to help me disentangle my legs and check my shoulder bandage. I feel better after she rubs my ears. I move forward planting one paw in the greening grass after the other. What's so silly about a goose, I wonder. The last one I sniffed chased me out of my own yard. "I don't want to do this," I whine. "I don't want to go for a walk." I sit down in the center of the pavement on the sunset road.

Elizabeth doesn't notice until she's almost around the curve. I've been willing her to stop and turn back since we began. It takes her a long time to recognize my signal and act on it. She comes back, rubs my neck and we both amble home.

The days drone on. I watch as rabbits come and go with the sun. I barely eat or move. The crows take my biscuits that Elizabeth sets out for me. Good. I'm tired and I don't want trouble from that flock. When I get up to pee I can't lift my leg like Beau taught me. I squat. Gradually the pain bites less and I move around our yard. I'm not ready to resume my duties until the moon is round.

During my next walk with Elizabeth we stop to see Beau. She talks with Mrs. Schmidt while I plant my stiff body beside my old friend. He's tangled in a roll of white tape. It starts on his back leg, stretches up and over a white cover on his rear haunches than wraps around his leg, loops under his belly and around his tail.

"Hey."

"Come in Herbie." Beau coughs whenever he talks so we try to keep his part of the conversation brief. "I feel as lost … cough… as a fish…cough, cough… on my alpha's cleaning board…cough, cough, cough."

"That good? Are you aware you have bandages everywhere, especially on your rump? Does your poop chute still work?" I say.

That makes him laugh, and cough. "It didn't for a vhile," he says.

"Herbie," says Elizabeth. "We should go home. Beau needs his rest."

"Bojo, Beau." I join Elizabeth and we amble down the sunrise road.

Two suns later I walk by myself to see Beau Schmidt. I stand at the edge of his kingdom and wait for permission to enter.

"Herbie, I sense birds in these trees. I can't move or see. What kind are they?"

I scan the sycamore and white pine in his yard. "Don't worry, Beau. No owls are lurking over you. Your luck has turned. You need to concentrate on healing your butt so we can go exploring in the swamp again."

"Not me. I'm staying clear of that"…cough, cough. "Did Bob really punch out the driver of that van that hit me?" Beau says.

"Knocked him flat. Then he made him help carry you to his trunk."

"His trunk? Bob let me ride in his car?" Beau says.

"His back seat and trunk are stained with blood, yours and mine."

"Bob let both of us ride in his immaculately clean car? The man is full of surprises. I didn't think he liked me," Beau says.

"He doesn't. Where did all these bones come from?" I say scanning the yard. "Are you expecting guests or will you eat them all yourself?"

"Help yourself," Beau says. "My alpha gives them to me. He says since I'm an older dog I need to eat different foods to keep strong. He says older dogs can't bark as loud, move as fast, or pee as high so they don't need as much strength or as much food as they once needed. He says older dogs need softer bones because their teeth get vorn down. He says older dogs like me can expect to feel more pain so the food comes vith medicine already mixed in."

"It sounds like becoming an older dog could be worse than becoming bloated road kill. Maybe it's smarter to die when we are younger dogs."

"No, Herbie. A longer life is better. If you died young who vould chase all these squirrels? Who vould vatch over Elizabeth? Who vould teach visdom to Bob? Who vould remember the legends? No, you must stay alive. But, I've decided how to deal vith growing old."

"How's that?" I ask.

"Stop listening to my alpha."

I laugh. "The doctor may be right about eating to gain strength. Why not try one of these juicy bones before I eat them all?"

"I fight the gag reflex each time I try. I'm just not hungry."

I notice Beau seems smaller, although it's hard to tell with all his bandages. He's still wrapped like a Potawatomi papoose. I take a juicy looking t-bone with meat and cartilage clinging to its sides. I chew down and smack my lips. "Beau you should try to eat one like this."

"As good as all that?" Beau asks.

"Delicious. It's not just mouth-watering. I'm upgrading the flavor to flash flood status. Are you sure you won't join me?"

Beau doesn't answer. He's trembling. I can hear a ticking sound as his head moves. He's staring straight ahead and shaking like a bead in a rattle.

"Beau, are you trying to scare me?" I say.

No answer. He falls over on his side. His body jerks.

"Woof, woof, woof!" I bark. "Someone help Beau! Woof, woof, woof." I freeze. I can't move."Woof, woof, woof."

Recognizing the distress call, Doctor Schmidt rushes from his garage. "What's going on?" he says. When he sees Beau writhing on the dead grass, he slows and walks to his side.

I begin to shake.

"Calm down, Herbie. He'll be all right. Beau is having a seizure. There's nothing we can do until it's over."

He tries to rub me calm, but my muscles are in knots. I've never seen my friend like this before.

"It's okay, boy." Doctor Schmidt rubs my ears. "The accident seems to have brought back the seizures he had as a pup," he tells me. He's still rubbing my neck when the trembling stops and Beau settles into a deep sleep. "Go home, Herbie. Your friend needs to rest."

I back from his yard keeping Beau in full view, then turn and stagger home. I wonder if Doctor Schmidt is right. I would jump in the lake with the underwater wolf if I lost another best friend.

Walks Like a Bear, you are wondering about Beau Schmidt?

"Wolf, I needed you."

I've been busy, but then, so have you. Remember what Calle said about losing hope?

"I do, and Beau's guardian said he would be all right. Wolf, I'm so angry with the driver who hit Beau. I swear I wouldn't pee on him if he was on fire."

FORTY-FIVE

Tonight I sit listening before the fire. I can hear Bob and Elizabeth discussing the bait shop and party store that a family wants to build across the lake on Eagle Point.

"Neighbors are angry," says Elizabeth. "This lake was carved out of the landscape by a glacier thousands of years ago. They don't want to look out their windows and see unnatural lights flickering from a party store. I have been asked to sign a petition."

"Did you sign?"

"No. I've talked to the People who want to build and operate the store. They are Native American, Potawatomi, from the same clan that was driven from this area 163 years ago."

"History does move in a circle," Bob says. "So, you don't mind looking out at a bait shop?"

"Of course I do. I'd rather we had the only cottage on this lake and there were no loud boats or jet skis, except for ours, of course. Herbie, what's wrong with you?"

"What does he want now? Why is he nosing your leg and licking you?" says Bob. "Does he want another cookie?"

"Bob, I think he agrees with me. I think he wants to see the Potawatomi move back to Clark Lake."

I wiggle my butt and bark. She gets it. She understands. The woman is capable of learning. I wonder if I can teach her the legends.

Walks Like a Bear.

"Hello, Wolf."

Show her. She can learn.

"Herbie," Bob says. "If your breeders could have known how smart you would become, they would have charged Elizabeth double." He turns to his wife. "This is an intelligent sheep dog, Elizabeth; he agrees with you. He could be a genius if he would only agree with me."

FORTY-SIX

During the moon when the snow blows spirits in the wind, warm weather sometimes brings a welcome thaw, a celebration of joy, a hint of spring. It never comes easily. It starts with a drizzle that drools into rain that becomes a downpour that evolves into miserable, wet, gray Michigan mud.

I lay next to a puddle watching drips ripple into rings like training collars. The rain stops. It's during this rare pause of sunshine that the lake develops ground fog. The snow, layered high on top our cottage, melts, then roars down the roof tiles and crashes into heaps of slush on the patio below.

Mud oozes from between my toes as I walk the familiar paths. If I keep my nose low I can see the first peas poke up in the garden, newly arrived to daylight. The sun gives fuel to flowers, gives anticipation for long sleeps in sunshine, and gives the expectation of flocks of visiting ducks and geese migrating still further north. It gives me hope for the appearance of the sand hill crane, the last bird to arrive and bring with it the summer season. This break in weather is the best time to lie on patio bricks, smell oozing pine pitch and think of the dream of my youth, my destiny.

I only remember one dream that is significant: I become a father and teach my pups all I know. It is a pleasant dream, but impossible. I can never be a father. My destiny is off to a slow start.

Two wax-scented shoes arrive in the patio fog as I stir from where I'm enjoying my morning musings. His familiar male scent is filled with so much power that I pause from counting drips from the melting roof snow. When Bob clears his throat I am reminded this man can be dangerous. His loafers are buffed to brilliance and decorated with shiny copper pennies that slide inside a leather pocket on each arch. They have come to rest on the bricked patio no more than two steps from my nose. I smell trouble.

I try to ignore the shoes, but there is a bright smear of mud, the merest sniff tells me it is excrement. I am intrigued in spite of myself, though I refuse to lift my eyes.

A gruff voice speaks from somewhere above the shoes, deep and resonant, with authority. It is while he's speaking that I hear the first crack in the roof snow from above.

"Herbie," the voice says in a controlled whisper, a monotone. "Use the O'Riley woodlot." He pauses and moves his voice up a pitch. The cuffs of his wool trousers are stiffly pressed into perfect jutting prows. I hear the faintest creak of tendon and patella, and then the knees present themselves. A fist is pressed to the patio not a paw's width from my nose. It smells bad, like soap. The man leans in close. I can smell his breath, terrible, like mint. I hear the snow creak. I hear the softening ice begin its long slide down the roof tiles, slowly at first. It picks up speed as it nears the edge.

"Find a spot in Elizabeth's rose garden."

I edge backwards, beyond the patio bricks, onto the dormant lawn.

His smile is a sneer. His whisper goes up in volume. "Use the outhouse." He punches each whispered word as it erupts from his mouth. "But, do not defecate where I walk." The whisper vanishes. So does the smile. He threatens me in a voice loud enough to be heard across the lake. "Next time I will rub your nose in it!"

The shoe leather squeaks as his body straightens. The shoes swivel towards the cottage. "Elizabeth!" he barks at full volume towards the kitchen door. "If this beast does not learn toilet manners he is going back to Ken-Bear's kennel." His hands go up on his hips to emphasize his decision is final.

Bob shouldn't have looked up when he heard the roar. He shouldn't have left his mouth open.

"Elizabeth?" the alpha whines, coated in slush that soaks his head and shoulders. The sludge from the roof wilts his trousers and invades his shoes. The copper pennies in the waxed loafers disappear beneath a swirl of slop.

Elizabeth answers his pitiful wail. She stifles laughter as she opens the door. "Pull those pants off. Leave them outside. Leave the shoes too!" The woman brushes hunks of ice from his shoulders and peels his soaking shirt away, pulling it off by its cuffs. Bob shivers like a butterfly fresh from its cocoon while Elizabeth scurries to locate his robe. "Bob, if you'd hang this up instead of dropping it on…"

"Elizabeth! I'm freezing out here," he shudders.

I howl to the stars in the midnight sky. *Calle, can you see me?*

Elizabeth is laughing as she towels ice from his hair. "Come inside the kitchen." A southwester slams the door shut behind him with a bang.

I can see you, says Wolf. *Red Dog is up here with me.*

Bojo, Walks Like a Bear, says Calle O'Riley. *We will both be watching you from behind these stars. Would you do a favor for your old mentor?*

"Anything," I say.

Protect the O'Riley pack until they can find another dog, she says.

"I will do as you ask. And I will use all you have taught me to honor the People and the animals so we don't destroy our world."

Will you run away again if you get in trouble or if your life seems too hard? says Wolf.

I laugh. "Good luck brought me to Clark Lake. Patience will help me with Bob. I want to spend the rest of my seasons with this family. I will stay, no matter what happens. Bojo Wolf. Calle, I'm sorry I didn't fight Eagle when you asked for my help."

Don't be sorry. I wasn't looking forward to starving and I always wanted to fly. It was the best way for me to get to the afterworld. Thank you for being a good student.

"Calle, I miss you. You were my best friend."

I am still your friend up here. I can see you. Do you see the star blinking at you from the sky? That's me. Look a little more in this direction. That's it. Can you see me now?

"I see you blinking. Remember to watch over me. Will you seal our deal for luck?" I say, stretch, circle three times around and settle down in the patio fog to wait for the next shooting star.

THE END

Laurice LaZebnik has a BS in Education from Central Michigan University. LaZebnik taught secondary school Art and English, worked in international marketing and sales and in the local community as a volunteer. A licensed pilot and real estate salesperson, the author balances a social life with her husband with caring for elderly parents and her two dogs. She currently cheers and hoots for Herbie the Love Bug who is a Bronze Level Grand Champion Old English sheepdog, so far...